Overcoming
Performance
Anxiety

REALIZATIONS

• I HAVE THIS WHOLE THING BACKWARDS. IT IS A CHANCE TO SHINE, NOT A CHANCE TO FAIL !!!

• I SHOULD START SMALL AND RISE UP.

• I REALLY GOT HAMMERED SOMEWHERE ALONG THE WAY, BUT THAT DOES NOT MATTER NOW !!!

Overcoming Performance Anxiety

Rod and Eversley Farnbach

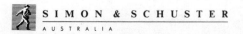

SIMON & SCHUSTER
AUSTRALIA

First published in Australia in 2001 by
Simon & Schuster (Australia) Pty Limited
20 Barcoo Street,
East Roseville NSW 2069

A Viacom Company
Sydney New York London Toronto Tokyo Singapore

National Library of Australia
Cataloguing-in-Publication Data

Farnbach, Rod.
    Overcoming performance anxiety.

    Bibliography.
    Includes index.
    ISBN 0 7318 0798 7

    1. Performance anxiety. 2. Rational-emotive psychotherapy.
    3. Speech anxiety. 4. Self-help techniques. I. Farnbach,
    Eversley. II. Title.

616.85223

Set in Stone Serif 10/13pt
Cover design by Greendot Design
Internal design by DiZign
Typeset by Asset Typesetting Pty Ltd
Printed in Australia by Griffin Press

10 9 8 7 6 5 4 3 2 1

Contents

Introduction

For much of the time we are awake, we are doing things. Some things we find hard to do, others we find easy. Some things are important, some trivial, some familiar, some strange.

And all the time we think. We think about ourselves and others, and about past, present and future events. We never stop thinking. Because we think, we can be afraid of not doing well enough. We can worry about failing. If we can worry about failing, we can have performance anxiety.

Almost everything we do can be done well or not well, or can be failed at altogether. Given the human condition, you can bet that someone, somewhere, is anxious about how well or badly they are doing things.

Few people have never experienced performance anxiety. Most of us undergo it in one or two areas of our lives and are hardly aware of it. But some people are so severely affected by performance anxiety that they live miserable and fearful lives. For example, if you fear public speaking but rarely do it, you have a very small problem. But if you have to speak publicly often, you will be terrified much of the time.

Performance anxiety is a nasty and pervasive human condition. It causes fear before and during a performance (defined here as doing almost anything at all), and misery afterwards. It also often causes anger at oneself. It is responsible for low confidence, depression, drug and alcohol abuse, blighted or unstarted careers, and impaired performance in numerous areas of activity. It is responsible for difficulties in social encounters, sex and romance, marriage and parenting, and sports and the arts.

In short, it interferes with almost every activity where it is possible for one to do well or badly, or to fail completely. It sounds like an epidemic because it is one.

This book employs the philosophy, theory and methods of Rational-Emotive Behaviour Therapy (REBT), originated by Dr. Albert Ellis around 1955, and developed since then. REBT is based on the knowledge that it is how we think about the events of our lives, not the events themselves, that determine our emotions (feelings) and actions. This explains why different individuals can, and will, feel differently in response to the same event. The 1st century AD Greek Stoic philosopher Epictetus stated, 'People are disturbed not by things but by the view they take of them.' He was right.

Dr. Ellis was the first of the modern cognitive behaviour therapists. Since 1955, several schools of cognitive behaviour therapy (CBT) have emerged, developed by Aaron Beck, Donald Meichenbaum and others. REBT is now established as one of the world's most effective and widely practised therapies.

REBT theory maintains that if we feel disturbed and/or are behaving contrary to our reasonable interests, we need to make our thinking logical and rational in order to feel and to perform better. Distressing emotions such as anger, anxiety and misery are caused by irrational thinking that defies fact and logic. For example, believing that to bore or disappoint one's audience would be awful, unbearable and proof that you are a total failure would be quite enough to cause severe public-speaking phobia (and it does). It would be better to replace this belief with the more sensible belief that you are, on the evidence, unlikely to cause such displeasure, and further, that whatever happens would be bearable, and logically incapable of proving that you are a failure (or anything else). Such beliefs, if strongly held, would make it impossible for public-address terror to occur.

REBT theory also concedes the undeniable, including that we have a past, and that our past experiences influence us in the present. But it emphatically rejects the idea that our past controls us now. This is a practical point, as the past cannot be changed. What can be changed is how we think about it now. REBT does this efficiently, meaning effectively and with a fair economy of time and effort.

In practice, REBT:

- focuses on present events, mainly but not exclusively;
- assumes that emotional disturbance is caused by a particular pattern of thoughts (self-talk);
- assumes that the self-talk is an expression of a personal philosophy such as 'I must succeed, because if I don't I'm a failure';
- assumes — in fact — knows, that this philosophy and self-talk, in order to cause fear and avoidance, must be illogical. Such beliefs, because they cause emotional pain and self-defeating behaviour, are referred to as 'irrational';
- expects that the irrational beliefs that cause performance anxiety will almost certainly include:
  (a) a belief that that one must succeed; and/or
  (b) a belief that one must be accepted and approved of; and/or
  (c) a belief that anxiety symptoms that are awful and unbearable, and ensure that peak (or even adequate) performance is made impossible; and
  (d) a conviction that to fail (or merely not do well), is evidence that one is a failure, a lesser person;
- identifies irrational beliefs in the individual — each person has his own special pattern;
- by a process of disputing the factuality, logic and utility of these beliefs, demonstrates that they are destructive and irrational;
- helps us to replace irrational beliefs with new, rational (verifiable, logical, flexible, coping and self-enhancing) beliefs;
- encourages the use of exercises, including behavioural challenges, to reinforce the adoption of the new belief system.

You may have a problem with all this. Possibly, you are pretty happy with your life, but have specific, isolated performance anxiety in just one area, such as career, sport, study, arts performance or public speaking. You may see this as a technical problem, and not like the idea of needing therapy. 'There's nothing wrong with me; I just have a problem with ...'

The fact is that REBT has varied applications, not just for treating neuroses and personality problems, but for training and education, in business and in industrial relations and for sports performance enhancement. Our advice is that you see the application of REBT (which, by the way, is based on a solid scientific foundation and not on untested theories) as an aspect of training, mental preparation and toughening up. Why 'toughening up'? Because learning to cope with anxiety, and pressing on despite the risk of failure, makes you mentally tougher, and more likely to gain the satisfaction of achieving your long- and short-term goals.

Performance anxiety, whatever the cause, whoever the victim, and regardless of what activity is involved, can be overcome. We have seen this happen in practice, and there is plenty of experimental evidence to confirm these observations. We can't guarantee that these methods and this book will help you, but if you apply yourself, and have a bit of patience, you will probably get over your performance anxiety, and experience more enjoyment and success in achieving your goals.

How to use this book. Simply start on the next page, and read and work to the end. You may find it helpful to complete the questionnaire in Chapter 19 after reading Chapter 4. This will give you not only a general understanding of the irrational beliefs that trouble people, but, also, some idea of which ones specifically affect you. This knowledge may help to direct your attention. But do not exclude seemingly irrelevant topics.

Chapter 19 — The Quick Fix. Some readers may have a performance challenge soon, and not enough time to read the whole book. If this is your situation, go straight to Chapter 19 and be directed by it. This abbreviated approach will almost certainly be appreciably better than doing nothing. Once the performance challenge is over, remember that life will have more such treats for you down the track, and start working on the book thoroughly — do 'The Slow Fix'.

1 Anxiety and Performance

This book is not about winning or even how to succeed. It is about overcoming the anxiety that stops so many people from doing what they want to do, taking even small risks and reaching their potential in many areas of their lives.

Everyone has heard of anxiety, and has some idea of what it is. But they don't usually talk of being anxious, or think of themselves as being anxious. They are much more likely to say they are apprehensive, panicky, afraid, scared, freaked out, terrified, or whatever their favourite expression is. These words all mean the same thing — being anxious.

Fear or anxiety?

Fear and anxiety are not the same. Fear refers to perceiving that you are in danger. For example, if you meet a large, bad-tempered bear while walking in the woods, you will experience fear.

Anxiety is your response to fear — apprehension, heightened vigilance, hyperventilating, dilated pupils, sweating, a racing pulse and running faster than a speeding bear.

This is a primitive response to a primitive situation. It is known as the fight-or-flight response — the mental and physical survival mechanism that prepares us to stand and fight, or to escape. (See Chapter 2, 'Understanding Anxiety').

Note the word 'primitive'. In our society we rarely meet real physical danger, but we often inappropriately activate the survival response of anxiety, and we have allowed ourselves to perceive safe situations as dangerous, and to predict that non-harmful things happening today will have harmful future consequences. Our minds create the danger, and we respond with the survival reaction, anxiety, as if we are in real physical danger.

We have learned to believe that some situations might lead to the loss of our wellbeing, comfort or reputation, and that this would be extremely harmful. So it is possible to take a situation that is not at all dangerous, a performance situation, such as giving a lecture to an audience who might become bored, and trick yourself into perceiving danger. You react by becoming anxious. This all happens because of the way you think about the situation, and through asking yourself the question 'What if ...?' The response to that question can involve drastic words and images, and related doubts about your ability to cope with the situation.

In practice, the distinctions between these words are flexible. The word 'fear' is not used only to mean a perception, but is also often used to describe the feeling. People often talk of feeling fear, meaning anxiety. We will follow the vernacular use at times, confident that you will know what we mean.

Few of us escape performance anxiety

Performance covers just about anything we do, from baking a cake or talking to a new neighbour to performing a cello concerto with the Berlin Philharmonic.

Anxiety about performance is extremely widespread, and can intrude into almost any human activity. Many adults or children (we start learning early how to give ourselves a hard time), when given a task or challenge, will become anxious. The result may be a tentative and inadequate performance or one of high quality. There may be procrastination, or complete avoidance. The cost always includes the discomfort of anxiety, and sometimes depression. Completing the task may bring relief, but what about the next time, and times after that?

Performance anxiety is ubiquitous, and few of us escape it completely. Think of someone you know who is truly confident, quietly so, without any arrogance, and who never boasts about or belittles their own performance, who admires the successes of others and is pleased for them, who competes vigorously without being over-competitive, who likes to succeed and tries hard to do so, but can calmly accept failure or loss. You are thinking of a rather unusual person. We can more likely identify, in some ways at least, with the people below, who will feature further in the book.

John — concert pianist

John is 44 years old, and is a highly regarded concert pianist. But he has a secret problem. Every time he performs, he is terrified because he fears he will not play 'perfectly'. Naturally, he hardly ever performs to his idea of perfection, so he goes on being terrified, pursuing the impossible. He believes he must continue giving concerts — after all, he has much to offer — so he must also continue to suffer the inevitable terror. Trying to play perfectly is bad enough, but having to do so while being alarmed and distracted by head pressure, tight breathing and shaky hands means that poor John really has to struggle to survive each concert.

John performs at a very high level. To continue in his career, he must please his audiences, and this involves playing at a high standard. His problem is that he does not know where to draw the line, how to discriminate between perfection (whatever that is) and what is good enough for ordinary mortals. He strives in all areas of his life to meet unreachable standards. For all his intelligence, he can't see that these standards exist only in his imagination. However well he does, he always believes he could do better. He is also a hypochondriac, because he has to be in perfect health in order to play perfectly, or so he believes.

Anne — lawyer

Anne is 35 years old, and in the 12 years since she graduated at the top of her year in law school she has done well in her career. She has worked for several well-regarded law firms, and has never had to apply for any job. Her associates and clients like her pleasant manner and her competence, empathy and profession-alism. She is a good advocate, and because of this she is often in court. She does it well and is often successful. At school she was in the senior debating team, and even then she noticed that when it was time to speak, she had butterflies in her stomach and her hands shook. She thought it was natural, perhaps caused by sleeping poorly the night before. However, her anxiety has insidiously grown worse, and nowadays it troubles her for a day or so before each case. What she notices most is the fluttering and churning in her stomach and, occasionally, nausea. Just before she goes into court it is worst, and sometimes she vomits before she appears. She gets through the court hearings only because she is so absorbed in the arguments and the proceedings. Practising meditation has not reduced her courtroom anxiety.

It is just as well that Anne loves her work and that the rest of her life is in good order; she notes with interest that she can give talks comfortably. In court, however, before her legal colleagues, more is riding on her performance. She and her skills are on display. She loves what she does, but it's her work, her livelihood. She has the talent and she is successful, so what is she afraid of?

She is making the mistake of overvaluing the occasion, the outcome, and what her clients and legal colleagues think of her.

She would agree that nobody's life is perfect and hers is pretty good, yet she seems to believe that one slip in court, one 'sub-perfect' performance, will demolish all she has in her favour.

Tom — student

Tom is a 20-year-old student who frustrates and disappoints himself, his family and his lecturers. They all know he is bright (he is beginning to doubt this), but his performance at school and university has been marred by his lack of concentration and effort, and his tardiness with assignments. He tries to concentrate on his studies, but he also wants to socialise a lot, so not much work gets done.

He jokes about these problems but they do worry him. He knows that his reliance on coffee, beer, cigarettes and marijuana doesn't help, but he can't cut down on them. He puts off almost everything. He recently missed an opportunity to date a girl who was obviously interested in him, as he was anxious about asking her out, and delayed too long. His mother read about Attention Deficit Disorder in a magazine, and thought 'That describes Tom', but she is wary about diagnosing the 'disorder of the month' and of discussing it with him.

There are many students who, like Tom, cannot manage to live up to their potential. They frequently suspect, often correctly, that they are more capable than many others who don't have any difficulty in seeing a challenge, facing up to it, working and getting solid results. Something stops people like Tom from achieving what they want in almost all areas of their lives. They don't necessarily perceive or admit their anxiety. They say they can do what needs to be done — studying, applying for a job, learning a new task, asking for a date — but they just don't get around to it, or if they do, they are late. They muck around, procrastinating; they find other things that 'must' be done first. They do anything but get on with the job. The result is lost opportunities and unrealised potential.

Susan — homemaker, wife and mother

Susan is a 36-year-old woman, wife of George and mother of Melissa, a quiet 14-year-old schoolgirl. George works long hours running his pharmacy, longer than he would like, but they need the money. It would help if Susan was employed, but she gave up her office job as soon as she knew she was pregnant. Now she spends her day running the household, which she does capably, and socialising a little with three old school friends.

Susan did well at school, but was always nervous and shy, and left when she was 15. She worked for the same employer for seven years. He liked her personally and valued her reliability, but he wished she had more initiative. Everyone likes Susan, seeing her as agreeable, although rather dull company.

Susan never takes any risks. She made excuses to avoid returning to work, and she refuses all invitations to join committees, so she is no longer asked. Although Susan loves children, Melissa was destined to be an only child, as Susan always believed that this was all she could cope with.

Susan is pleasant, but not a lot of fun. She always feels tense and doesn't sleep well. George was pleased when their doctor recently started her on antidepressant medication. He hopes it will help her to become calmer, happier and more confident, and hopes that their social life will improve, as Susan has always made excuses to refuse party and dinner invitations. If she accepted, she would have to return the favour and she dreads the thought of putting on a dinner party. She did once, years ago, and was in a state of 'nervous exhaustion' for days afterwards, although everyone enjoyed themselves.

You may know someone like Susan. She is fairly severely affected, but the elements are the same for all people with her problem. She is shy, socially anxious, and afraid of displeasing people by not doing well at something. Someone might not like her cooking, her conversation or her personality, so she plays it safe by avoiding taking social risks. Ironically, her attempts to avoid displeasing people have an effect opposite from what she wants. Even George, who loves her, wishes that her interests were not so restricted and safe.

Susan's doctor might be unwittingly treating social phobia (significant anxiety about being with, or talking to, people), as well as depression.

Gordon the Golfer

Gordon loves his golf, but he loves to win even more; so much so that he believes he must win. He belongs to a club, plays off a low handicap, and sometimes makes it into the pennant team. He has a bag of clubs so heavy that he practically needs a horse to carry it. He plays every Saturday and Sunday and any other time he can get away from work. He also has as many lessons as he can manage.

His fellow club members might possibly be amused by his obsession, but he is unpleasant to play with. Everyone has stories about his 90-decibel profanity and club-throwing, arguments over rules and scores; some even suggest quietly that he cheats when he thinks he can get away with it.

Golf is not his only problem. In work, recreation, or anything else, Gordon is intensely competitive. His wife and children, and the employees in his small engineering firm, find his nit-picking and criticism hard to take. Although they respect his energy and high standards, they consider his arrogance and bad temper distasteful. He boasts about his inability to 'suffer fools gladly', and about how he does not believe in 'taking prisoners'. He often scathingly refers to other people as 'losers'.

Gordon has the material trappings of success, and is good at golf and most of the things he does (after all, he does work hard at it), but he is not doing so well at being happy. His whole life is like his golf; any new task, any contest, and Gordon becomes so tense and irritable that people know to keep out of his way. When he succeeds, he is exultant, in fact he gloats, and when he fails (as he sees it), he is miserable for days. However, his fellow golfers are almost pleased that he is the way he is; they know that if he relaxed and enjoyed himself, he would be a far better golfer than they could ever be.

Gordon manages to enjoy neither the game of golf nor the game of life. He believes that anything less than success is failure, and the worth of a person, any person, is determined by whether the person succeeds or fails at significant tasks. Of course it is Gordon who is the judge of what constitutes success or failure, and whether someone is worthwhile or not. He is frequently arrogant and unpleasant to others because he applies the same standards to them as he does to himself. In any contest, his own self-worth is on the line, which puts him in real danger (he thinks). No wonder he becomes depressed when he loses a challenge. The danger never goes away, because no matter how well he has done before, there is always the future waiting to ambush him.

Julie — high school student

Julie is 16 years old and preparing for her final year school examinations. She is very anxious about them as they will determine whether or not she can get into medical school. She has always worked hard and obtained very good results.

Consequently her parents (both doctors) expect her to do well at the forthcoming exams and follow them into the medical profession.

Julie is keen to study medicine but is not confident that she will do well enough to qualify for entry. Because she works very hard, she is always tired. She tells her relatives and others that she, like her school friends, must work until midnight nearly every night of the week. She is beginning to feel miserable and even a bit ill — as though she is coming down with a mild virus — but she must keep going because the exam week (and her future) is drawing closer.

Julie has imposed a set of demands, in the form of standards and expectations, on herself. Her parents have done well enough in their careers, and they hope that their daughter will have a happy life, including a career that she enjoys and that will earn her enough. They haven't imposed any standards on her. She took their hopes, and turned them into demands. They think 'It would please us if Julie did well academically', and Julie thinks 'I must please my parents by doing well academically and take up medicine as a career.'

This is bad enough for her, but she is at risk of generalising from these demands to 'I want to please everybody by doing well at everything.' The threat to her self-worth is such that she suffers from anticipatory anxiety, impaired performance, and depression if she under-performs.

What the cases tell us

We have described six cases, different people who experience performance anxiety in varying situations. Perhaps you can see some common themes running through all these cases, although each has its own characteristics. Susan, for instance, might find it hard to believe that she and Gordon have similar problems, and he would certainly ridicule any suggestion that he and a 'loser' like Susan had anything in common. The thread that ties them all together is, of course, the fact that each person exhibits performance anxiety in one of its many manifestations.

Performance anxiety is widespread

Performance anxiety affects people from all backgrounds. It operates in all areas of life, whether it be someone's occupation, recreation, the sports they play, the arts they practise, personal relationships or just day-to-day living. For example, it is extremely common for people to be anxious about presenting for a job interview, or starting in a new job, dating someone they want to impress, doing an examination, or beginning a new venture.

Sports

Sportspeople of all standards often experience performance anxiety. Golfers are subject to 'the yips', their term for the common disorder of uncoordinated arm movements when putting. Some famous golfers are well known for losing concentration and playing badly at a certain stage of a tournament, or on a particular course, or when the ball is in a particular lie. Tennis players can have trouble with their serve, their backhand or some other stroke, because of anxiety.

At the very highest levels of sport, there is not much to separate competitors as far as skill is concerned, and very often what makes one player win over another is his or her confidence on the day. There are numerous instances of famous players who have a 'bad patch' that lasts for weeks or months, or sometimes long enough to wreck the player's career.

The arts

Performance anxiety is rife in the world of the creative arts, and it afflicts amateurs and highly gifted professionals alike — talent provides no protection. Sir Laurence Olivier, the great English actor, spent some years absent from the stage, due to performance anxiety. The great pianist Vladimir Horowitz was famous not only for his brilliant playing, but for his fear of performing, with cancelled concerts and extremely long (up to ten years) absences from the stage. For a while, he would not perform unless he could see his doctor sitting in the front row. This was because he was afraid of being overwhelmed by whatever anxiety symptom terrified him the most. Very late in life he lost his anxiety, and even managed to enjoy performing.

Other leading musicians noted for suffering performance anxiety include the cellist Pablo Casals, and singers Luciano Pavarotti, Barbra Streisand and Carly Simon. Full marks to them — they acknowledged they had the problem. There are many others who are too ashamed of their perceived imperfection to be able to admit to anyone but their therapist and intimates that they have it.

❡ This sense of shame is intimately bound up with what the problem is all about, which is the need to be seen by others as being without fault. ❡

The workplace

The workplace is also a common setting for performance anxiety. People at all levels can be deeply afraid of criticism, including people high in the hierarchy, who cannot bear to have their utterances or decisions questioned by people working for them. Working too hard in order to do the very best possible job is so widespread that it has a name — 'workaholism'. Of course it is realistic for someone who likes their work or who may not get another job to be apprehensive about displeasing the boss and possibly being sacked, but that is not the issue here.

Parenting

To be a parent is to know the meaning of guilt and irrational self-blame, much of which is based on performance anxiety. Perhaps your friend's child is sitting up, walking, talking, sleeping through the night or passing any other milestone earlier than your own child. You're expected to be pleased about it, but you're not. Why is that? Performance anxiety.

There will be more opportunities later on, with children at school, learning music or ballet, or playing sport, for anxious parents to be overinvolved in how well their offspring are doing. Have you ever seen small children playing football, and heard the parents screaming on the sidelines? Some children are reduced to tears by this kind of pressure. It's all a symptom of performance anxiety, this time expressed through the child. The child's performance reflects on the parent's performance as a parent or coach.

From another angle, some parents are unable to praise their

children for succeeding in areas such as sport, schoolwork or university studies, working and making money, forming good relationships, or many other activities where they had failed to live up to the parents' own hopes. They are often pleased and proud for their child, but at the same time envious, and unable to praise the child for what she has achieved. Can you imagine this child's view of herself, and to what extent it increases the likelihood that she will later strive too hard or give up too easily?

Sex

People want to impress their partner when they go on a date, but sometimes this desire is so strong it causes extreme nervousness and inhibition. Slightly further down the track, it is common for people, especially men, to be anxious about their sexual performance. But it doesn't stop there. If a man cannot rise to the occasion, what does the woman do? She blames herself, for having failed to be attractive or exciting enough. Occasionally the poor man, having proved a minute before that he is a hopeless lover (his term, not ours), has to suffer the additional humiliation of a barrage of abuse from his lady friend, who until just a short time ago was about as friendly as it is possible to be. Why does she react this way? Do people become angry and abusive merely because of disappointment and frustration? Not at all. She is angry because she thinks he has just proved to her that she is not sexually attractive.

Higher education

Performance anxiety occurs in universities, as you might expect. Some lecturers fear lecturing, and avoid it. Many students procrastinate over starting or submitting assignments, and about one-third of postgraduate theses are not completed. Some will not speak up in tutorials for fear of saying something wrong and looking silly. Oral examinations terrify many people.

Public speaking

Public-speaking phobia is extremely common and is a powerful source of fear. Somewhat related is the inability, already mentioned, of many people to ask questions or make comments in seminars or meetings. There is obviously a strong social component to their anxiety and avoidance; they fear that their question could be a 'dumb' one, or their comment might be 'stupid' and so they would make a fool of themselves.

Where does it come from?

Performance anxiety is caused by thinking anxiously about some aspect of something one is going to do, about to do, or doing. Almost always, it boils down to believing that one's worth as a person is related to how well one does something. Our society encourages this belief; it values striving, always doing your best, competing, succeeding and winning. People are admired, revered, discounted or rejected according to how well or badly they do at this or that. Even if you don't succeed, you must always try your hardest, or be a moral leper. Parents, schools and community leaders believe this doctrine, and pass it on to children and young people. But also, there are some children who, unaided, decide that this is what they and their life are about.

It is often stimulating, and even enjoyable, to try hard, to compete and to do well. Obviously, success beats failure any day, but ask yourself:

(a) is there a natural law that says that we must strive, compete and win?

(b) if there is a law, then where does it come from?

(c) doesn't complying with the law impose a high cost of anxiety and misery?

There are benefits, such as higher standards in study, work and business, but these can be achieved just as well without self-torment. In any case, there are activities such as dating, mating and public speaking, where standards are irrelevant, and fear is obviously destructive.

Does losing performance anxiety mean that you would lose interest in an activity, not try, or not persist? Not a bit of it. Without performance anxiety you would be free of the fear that makes people procrastinate, half-try, perform below their capacity, and give up easily.

Do you have performance anxiety?

It is an uncommon person who is quite calm at the prospect of having to give an address or a lecture to a large number of people, or taking on an unfamiliar major task. We envy and admire such people because we see them as unusual. If we boldly tackle a large or adventurous project, we later look back with pleasure and surprise, and realise that just for once, we did not frighten ourselves into thinking that we might be out of our depth.

People who make a bold move and set themselves a high goal in business, study, or some creative activity, and who work hard and succeed, often then find who among their friends has performance anxiety. Some of their friends will be genuinely pleased for them, but others will begrudge them their success, attributing it to luck or some unfair advantage that they themselves lacked. They react this way because in many cases they could have done the same and succeeded just as well, but they lacked confidence. To be confident in this situation means being able to see yourself as able to do what is necessary and, more importantly, not being afraid of failing.

It means recognising the possibility of failing, but refusing to see failure as shameful and bad, only as regrettable. Such thinking is incompatible with performance anxiety.

Understanding Anxiety

Anxiety defined

For the purpose of this book, we will define anxiety as a state of heightened arousal of the mind and body, associated with a belief that the individual is at risk and that he has a diminished capacity to control what is happening, or might happen, to him. This state can vary in intensity from very mild to extremely severe. This applies in performance anxiety.

In all emotions, there are effects in the mind and on the body. These effects involve:

- feelings (the emotional component);
- mental functioning, which refers to how the mind is working;
- physiological (bodily) reactions; and
- behaviour.

In anxiety, the effects are:

1. Feelings — these include irritability, apprehension, uneasiness, fear, panic and terror.
2. Mental functioning — the mind can be racing, frozen, or disorganised and unable to concentrate or remember (think of an actor freezing on stage). There might be intrusive thoughts and images about an impending performance, such as 'I will never pass this exam', and images of sitting miserably in the examination room.

3. Physiological (bodily) reactions — there are two types:
   (i) Increased muscle tension, and sometimes overactivity. This may be localised (such as in the shoulders, chest or stomach), or general. The symptoms include shaking, jerky movements and poor coordination.
   (ii) Overactivity of the sympathetic nervous system, which is part of the autonomic (automatic) nervous system. This is responsible for controlling non-muscular bodily functions, such as temperature regulation, digestion, heart rate and sweating. Symptoms include shaking, sweating, palpitations, and intestinal and bladder disturbances.
4. Behaviour patterns — including restlessness, talking excessively or withdrawing, irritable behaviour and self-medicating with alcohol, tobacco, marijuana and other sedatives.

The symptoms of anxiety are uncomfortable, and very familiar to anyone with performance anxiety. When we experience any discomfort, including anxiety, we respond with an inborn drive to try to make ourselves feel better. Some of us try to diminish the threat or danger. Others remove themselves from the perceived threat — this is the basis of avoidance, which you will read about later on.

Anxiety can be acute or chronic, that is, of short or long duration. The symptoms of chronic anxiety are the same as those of acute anxiety, but less intense, and include sleep loss, poor energy, depressed mood, and lowered immunity.

What is the function of anxiety?

Anxiety is a warning system, like pain, or the cry of a baby in distress. It warns us of potential danger in our environment, and prompts us to take steps to protect ourselves and/or adapt — a survival mechanism for the human race.

The fight-or-flight response
As mentioned in Chapter 1, anxiety is an adaptation to potential danger, when the mind and body are made ready for fighting or running away — the 'fight-or-flight response'. For most of us, real dangers do not exist now, but we still activate this primitive response in performance and other situations, as though they are truly dangerous. Each time we do, we reinforce the probability

that we will react the same way in similar non-dangerous performance situations in future; subsequent reactions are likely to be stronger. To make matters worse, we worry between events, so we not only experience isolated peaks of anxiety, but prolonged discomfort which impairs the health of our minds and bodies; this is a protracted stress reaction that stresses the immune system, making us more prone to physical illnesses.

Arousal — excitement, anxiety and anger

The emotional and physiological (bodily) state of anxiety is one of increased alertness, energy and activity. Everything is wound up and going faster. We call this state 'arousal'. Arousal refers to a state of mental and physical stimulation. Of itself, it is neither good nor bad. It is a component of various emotional states, some of which are good, and some not. For example, consider the emotions of anxiety, excitement and anger.

- Excitement = arousal + rational thoughts e.g. 'Oh boy! I am really on top of this assignment now. I think I'm likely to pass or even better!' Children (and adults) can experience pleasurable anticipatory excitement at Christmas and birthdays.
- Pleasurable anticipation (mild excitement) = arousal + rational thoughts. For example, 'I've worked as hard as I can on this speech. It will probably go well. If not, that's how it is sometimes. Whichever way it goes, I'll learn more about how to do better next time.'
- Anxiety = arousal + negative thoughts about what is going to happen. For example, 'I will perform badly and they will all think I am stupid and hopeless, so I am. I should be doing something I can cope with, like watching a television game show.'
- Anger = arousal + demanding and condemnatory thoughts towards other people, oneself, or fate. For example, 'I shouldn't have to play this rotten piece. It's too hard. It's not fair!'

This leads us to a very significant point — *arousal is essential for good performance.*

We perform better if we are aroused by a sense of competition or a standard to be met. Runners trying for their best time are more likely to succeed if they are competing against someone who is hard to beat. A feeling of being keyed up, aroused, is necessary because it improves concentration, accelerates thinking, and improves coordination and reflexes. However, while we need some arousal to perform well, we definitely do not need to be afraid. So, 'I need to be under pressure to work well' is nothing more than a rationalisation.

Note: We prefer to use the word 'arousal' when referring to this state of being expectant, sharp, on your toes. We avoid the use of the word 'anxiety' and 'stress' in this context, because these words can imply that something bad is happening, or will happen, to you.

	Anxious Performance	Unanxious Performance
Thinking style before performance	Fears of failure and disapproval — probably both	Pleasurable anticipation. Seeing the occasion as a challenge that he/she can meet
Arousal before and at the beginning of the performance	High	Somewhat elevated
Focus of attention during the performance	Symptoms of anxiety, errors, possible signs of audience displeasure	The task and its technicalities. Ignoring or accepting bodily sensations such as heightened arousal. Coping with difficulties. Enjoying the occasion and the achievement.

Fig 2.1   *Anxious and unanxious performance styles*

When a person is anxious, he may perceive his symptoms of arousal as harmful. When speaking in public he may become more upset when he feels his heart pounding. On the other hand, when someone is experiencing 'good' arousal, and is excited or pleased because of thinking rationally, they will hardly notice their palpitations. If they do, they will not see it as a problem; it may even be welcomed. People speak with pleasure about being 'pumped up' or having an 'adrenalin rush'. Elite athletes experience the same arousal symptoms before an event as less successful performers. They accept them as normal pre-performance sensations, not at all harmful, and even necessary. Less successful athletes see the symptoms as bad, and are afraid of them.

Since it is our thinking (rational or irrational) that can make the difference between anxiety and beneficial emotional states, by learning the skills of thinking rationally, we can overcome performance anxiety.

The effects of excess arousal

There can be too much of a good thing. Excessive arousal interferes with peak performance. With the mind racing and full of intrusive and sometimes irrelevant thoughts, the performer can lose his focus. Imagine that you are a championship golfer needing to sink a two-foot putt in order to win an important tournament. This is not the time for great dreams of glory and visions of sacks of gold. What is needed is an intense focus on the task, and for the muscles to be relaxed enough for a smooth swing.

Fig. 2.2 expresses this nicely. It is named after two psychologists who described this principle graphically about 70 years ago.

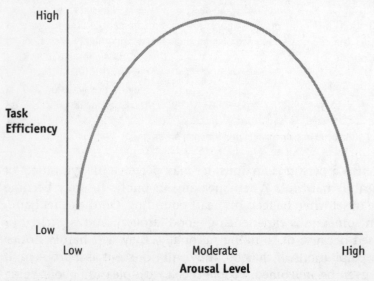

Fig 2.2 *Yerkes-Dodson Relationship*
(Note: This is not to any scale, and there are no units of arousal or efficiency.)

It shows that as arousal increases, concentration improves, as does the quality of performance — up to a point. Beyond that point, the high point of the curve, any further increase in arousal leads to a deterioration in performance quality.

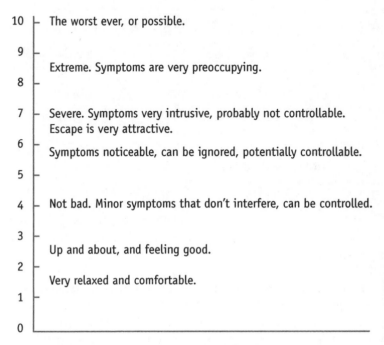

Fig 2.3   *Subjective Units of Discomfort Scale (SUDS)*

The scale refers to emotional and physiological discomfort as the person feels it, not what others observe. This reflects the fact that it is quite possible for someone to be extremely anxious, even having a panic attack, and for others to not notice that anything is wrong. To them, the person looks all right, but he is suffering. If he is in a panic attack, he is experiencing terror.

The scale is different for everybody. It is not precise, but it is constant for an individual.

You need to construct your own SUD scale, so start on that now. For two weeks, carry a small notebook, and observe your emotional reactions. Whenever you feel uncomfortable, and any other time that you think to do it, ask yourself what is your SUD and record it. At the same time, mentally check yourself for any symptoms of tension, tremors, feeling hot or cold, sweating or any other symptom of anxious arousal. After a couple of weeks you will have enough information about how you react to anxiety to enable you to construct your SUD scale.

Day/Date	Time, Events	SUDS	Symptoms
Mon 10/11	7.00 Dad in bad mood, nagging me.	5	Feel hot. Stomach and shoulders tight.
	3.00 Reading my work aloud in class.	6	Hot. Shoulders Stomach tight. Feel sick. Hands feel shaky.
	5.30 Archery practice, doing well. Feel keen.	4+	Stomach slightly tight.
Tues 11/11	5.30 Trying out for archery team.	6+	Hot. Stomach. Shoulders. Sick. Hands shaking.

Fig 2.4 *SUDS diary*

By first keeping a SUD scale, and then a SUD diary, you will soon recognise minor anxiety symptoms. This will give you a better chance to intervene with anxiety-reduction techniques. It is much harder to reduce anxiety when it is already high, at around 7 or more.

For instance, when you are very anxious, you might feel nausea or chest pain. This may indicate your SUD is 6.5 or so. Accurate self-observation, and constructing a SUD scale, is likely to teach you that before you develop strong, unpleasant symptoms, you feel mild tightness in your stomach or chest, or hand symptoms at a SUD of 4 or 5. Your own SUD scale will look like Fig 3.3, with physical symptoms attached at the various levels where they first occur.

Another good reason to use a SUD scale is that it is helpful to be able to observe (feel) your SUD falling as you apply coping techniques, such as meditation/relaxation, self-instructional training, self-hypnosis, auto-suggestion and worry management.

Avoidance

We have said that everybody's SUD scale is individual. There is one exception to this. There is something magical about the number 7. It signifies avoidance or the desire to avoid. That is, not going into a situation, leaving it prematurely, or pulling some stunt such as rushing a performance, in order to minimise engagement with it. In Rod Farnbach's (RWF) experience, without prompting, everyone discussing their avoidance estimates their SUDS to be 7 or more, and never less. One of your objectives is to never reach 7.

Avoidance is important because it is a very significant behavioural component of the anxiety response. We avoid in order to reduce, in the short term, our anxiety symptoms. It works quite well, as a rule, for a while. In the longer term, it leads to greater anxiety or a depressed mood. For fairly obvious reasons, it is not good for your self-respect to know that you are behaving in an ineffectual and 'scaredy-cat' manner.

Avoidance, as a coping technique, diminishes one's sense of control, and gives a sense of being controlled by events. The thinking is that there is something inherently bad in a situation, and the only way that you can feel any better is by getting out of there, and the sooner the better. Avoiding a feared situation perpetuates and intensifies the fear. It reinforces both the belief that your feelings cannot be coped with, and the tendency to think negatively about the circumstances, and about yourself. Avoidance establishes and maintains a vicious circle. It is rather like drinking alcohol to relieve anxiety.

Avoidance can be overt and obvious, such as not turning up for a performance or a contest, being too distressed to start or to continue, or leaving prematurely. The best-known form of avoidance, familiar to almost everybody, is procrastination (Ch. 13). Probably everybody does it to some extent, but some people dedicate their lives to procrastinating — or they would if they got around to it!

Covert avoidance, such as making elaborate preparations for an avoided task, or working on easier, semi-related but unnecessary tasks, is not obvious, and looks respectable to the avoider, and often to others.

Overt avoidance is much less likely to evoke sympathy and often draws criticism with a moralistic flavour.

To summarise, mild anxiety is normal, and although it is always uncomfortable, it is hardly ever harmful. Just the same, a little goes a long way, especially where performance is concerned. Some arousal is necessary in order to give a good performance. But too much arousal is uncomfortable, distracting and performance-impairing. The way out of the situation is to detect, challenge and change the irrational thinking that causes the anxiety, and apply the various coping strategies described later.

3 About REBT

Defining the word 'rational'

Rational thoughts, emotions and actions are those that enable us to achieve our realistic goals. Conversely, irrational thoughts, emotions and actions make it harder for us to achieve these goals. Although a group of people could probably generate a long list of worthwhile and realistic goals, we assume that most of these could be subsumed under the wish to lead a long and happy life.

That is the practical definition. Rational thinking is also logical, internally consistent, non-rigid and accords with known facts. We are always thinking, at least while we are awake. Just as our hearts beat without our conscious interference, so our brains are busy doing what they do. They think. We experience these thoughts as a stream of images or internal utterances. The term for this continual activity is self-talk.

In Rational Emotive Behaviour Therapy (REBT) we refer to the ABCs — the As, Bs and Cs — of an event:

- A = Activating event — something that happens;
- B = Beliefs which are activated by the activating event;
- C = Consequences — the emotional, physiological, mental functioning and behavioural responses (the way we feel emotionally and physically, how our minds work, and what we do) in response to B.

People tend to think and talk as if A causes C (A → >C). For example, 'Having to give a talk at the garden club (A) makes me nervous (C).' But this is wrong, and just as well, because if it were true it would mean that we never could do anything to change the way we react in a given situation. In fact, A activates B, which creates C, the consequences. The beliefs are expressions of our individual personal philosophical systems, and we experience the beliefs as our self-talk.

If the activated belief is rational, the emotion will be appropriate and controlled, and we will be more likely to act in our logical and reasonable self-interest. If the belief is irrational, we are more likely to have inappropriate, extreme or poorly controlled emotions, and thus to act self-defeatingly.

Let us consider this in more detail:

The activating events

Activating events (As) are:

- something we do, such as cheating at golf;
- something outside ourselves, done by another person, such as being told 'You bungled again, you dope!';
- something outside ourselves done by fate, and not by other people, such as having the computer crash for the umpteenth time;
- an internal physiological event, such abdominal pain or rapid heartbeats;
- an internal mental event, such as a memory, or daydreaming about being out on a date;
- even the mood we are in can be an activating event: we can be pleased about being in a good mood, upset about being irritable or unhappy, or anxious about being anxious.

Beliefs and personal philosophies

Beliefs are what we hold to be true, our attitudes and assumptions about success and failure, about love and acceptance or rejection, good or bad fortune, and other matters concerning ourselves and the wider world. They reflect our personal philosophies, which may be rational (verifiable, internally consistent and self-enhancing), or irrational (not verifiable, internally inconsistent and self-defeating).

When a belief is activated it gives rise to self-talk — the thoughts we experience in the moment. Self-talk creates the consequent mood and the associated physiological, mental and behavioural responses.

Hence A → >B (self-talk) → >C (happy, or depressed, or muddled thinking etc.)

Take the example of someone with examination performance anxiety:

- personal philosophy of the examination candidate — 'I must always succeed in order to be a worthwhile person.'
- belief (derived from the personal philosophy, and more specific): 'I absolutely have to do well in my chemistry exam.'
- self-talk (in the moments before the exam) 'I know I'm going to do badly. I won't be able to face anyone. I'll feel so ashamed.'

The self-talk is the starting point when we search for the underlying beliefs (Bs). These will lead us on to the personal philosophies.

It is the Bs which need to be changed in order to alter the emotional and behavioural responses or consequences.

So, when Jack and Jill don't win (A) the ballroom dancing competition, and Jack becomes depressed (C), it is because his Bs are negative and extreme:

JACK'S A → >B → >C
(A) 'Jill and I did not win the dancing competition.'
(B) 'We should have won. I'm a stumble-footed halfwit.'
(C) Jack feels depressed and miserable.

JILL'S A → >B → >C
(A) 'Jack and I did not win the dancing competition.'
(B) 'I wish we had won, but we can keep working on it and perhaps do better next time.'
(C) Jill feels only disappointment, and is motivated to try again.

Jack exaggerated the importance of the event, the benefits of winning, and the ill-consequences of losing. Jill did not exaggerate the importance of the event or 'awfulise' about the outcome, so she experienced only disappointment, not depression. If Jack is too depressed to join Jill in more dance practice, she may even have to find a new partner. More bad news for Jack.

The consequences

The consequences resulting from the activation of our beliefs, both rational and irrational are:
1. Emotional.
2. Physiological.
3. Mental.
4. Behavioural.

The major irrational emotional responses are:
- anxiety;
- depression;
- anger.

The rational counterparts of the irrational negative emotions are:
- concern;
- sadness;
- annoyance.

These rational responses are usually experienced as relatively mild and benign, as are their emotional, physiological, mental and behavioural accompaniments. They do not impair mental activity or goal-directed behaviour. Even when a rational negative response is severe, as in sadness, or acute grief, it feels 'right', appropriate, and not exaggerated and morbid.

The bodily (physiological), mental and behavioural consequences, both rational and irrational, are in keeping with the emotions.

Let us return to the activating events listed on page 28. Each of these As could activate either rational beliefs (rBs), or irrational beliefs (iBs), and lead to rational or irrational consequences. For instance:

1. *The golf cheat*
   (a) Rational belief — 'I wish I hadn't cheated. It was a mean thing to do, and I won't do it again.' Consequence — regret.

(b) Irrational belief — 'I shouldn't have cheated. I'm a mean sod.' Consequence — shame and guilt. Consequence — depressed mood.

2. *Being called a dope*
   (a) Rational belief — 'I don't like being called a dope. It's unpleasant. I wish he wouldn't abuse me.' Consequence — annoyance.
   (b) Irrational belief — 'He's a real pig! He has no right to talk to me like that.' Consequence — anger.
   (c) Irrational belief — 'He's right. I am incompetent. I'll never succeed at anything.' Consequence — depressed mood.
   (d) Irrational belief — 'It's awful when people criticise me. I can't stand it. He must be right about me. Everyone might reject me.' Consequence — anxiety.

3. *The computer crashes frequently*
   (a) Rational belief — 'This is a real nuisance. I'd better get the computer fixed.' Consequence — mild frustration.
   (b) Irrational belief — 'I can't stand it. This damned machine is no good. That swine who sold it to me is a crook.' Consequence — anger.

4. *Abdominal pain or rapid heartbeats*
   (a) Rational belief — 'I don't like this feeling. Perhaps I should drink less coffee. If it (my chest/stomach discomfort) doesn't improve, I'll see my doctor about it.' Consequence — concern.
   (b) Irrational belief — 'This has to be something terrible, like cancer or a heart attack. I know I'm done for.' Consequence — great fear (severe anxiety).

5. *Thinking of asking someone out on a date*
   (a) Rational belief — 'I'll ask her out. She wasn't very encouraging when I last met her, so she might knock me back. That doesn't seem so bad when I think about it. If she does, I'll find someone else.' Consequence — calm.
   (b) Irrational belief — 'I want to ask her out on a date, but what if she rejects me? Just thinking about it makes me ill. I feel like such a loser.' Consequence — anxiety and depression.

6. *Feeling irritable or 'flat' before a music audition*
   (a) Rational belief — 'I feel pretty flat today. But it happens to everyone. I will get over it. It won't stop me from auditioning this afternoon.' Consequence — neutral effect.
   (b) Irrational belief — 'Just my luck! The audition is this afternoon and I feel like this. I have to feel good in order to play well. I can't stand this horrible feeling.' Consequence — anxiety.

These examples illustrate some important points. These are:

* a given situation (A) can give rise to different emotional responses or consequences (C);
* these responses or consequences (C) can be irrational and disturbed, or rational;
* the type of response is determined by the type of belief (B) that is activated;
* iBs (irrational beliefs), in general, consist of demands on, and other unrealistic ways of thinking about, oneself, other people and life. By their unreasonable nature, they create disturbed feelings and other responses;
* rBs (rational beliefs) contain wishes and preferences, and give rise to undisturbed feelings and coping responses.
  This holds as a general principle.

And what about someone who is not experiencing any negative emotion? Such a person is happy and contented. That is the state that we default to when we are not experiencing any negative emotions. There is no mention of calmness; this is because a happy and contented person could be excited, which is an aroused state (remember the Yerkes-Dodson relationship?), and physiologically much the same as anxiety and anger.

Again, 'rational' thoughts, emotions and actions make it easier for us to achieve our realistic long-term goal of leading a long and happy life. 'Irrational' thoughts, emotions and actions make it harder for us to achieve this goal.

Case study — Judy and the garden club

Judy gave a talk about compost at her local garden club meeting today. Soon after she began to speak, she noticed that her good friend Jenny got up and left. Her thinking is rational if her self-talk is 'Jenny is very interested in compost, and she was keen to hear me speak today, so she must have left the meeting for a very good reason. Perhaps she was feeling ill or there was some other problem.' Judy has calmly considered the facts and looked for a reasonable, commonplace explanation.

An irrational response would be 'Jenny says she is a good friend of mine, so how could she have left the meeting when I was trying so hard to speak interestingly about compost! This happens to me all the time. People don't consider my feelings, and they treat me as if I'm unimportant. They must think I am boring, or irritating, or both.' This ignores the fact that Jenny has previously expressed genuine warmth towards Judy, the garden club meetings and compost.

It is not logical to draw radical conclusions about one's personality defects on the basis of what it is imagined that others think, particularly as there is no supporting evidence. Illogical thinking of that type is much more likely if the thinker holds irrational beliefs such as 'I'm not much of a person, and what worth I do have needs to be validated by other people, by their being nice to me at all times. This means they must never do anything to me that I would not like.'

It is plain that Judy's irrational self-talk is selective in its use of the facts, and illogically draws invalid conclusions. It displays an adherence to a troublesome personal philosophy, which is that she, Judy, must always be accepted and approved of by significant others. If she is in any way rejected or disapproved of, this tells her that she is a less worthwhile person. In other words, she is:

- demanding that she be liked and accepted by people who matter to her;
- measuring her worth as a person according to how much liking and acceptance she gets.

Although you may wonder how any intelligent person could hold such beliefs, it is a fact that just about all of us think this way to some extent. The irrational thinking that leads to performance anxiety is found in people who, regardless of their intelligence, have simply thought themselves into a state of emotional disturbance.

4 The Irrational Beliefs

The bad news about irrational beliefs is that the irrational thinker's disturbed thinking can impoverish his quality of life. In addition, innocent bystanders can be caught up in the anguish or anger of this person.

The good news is that there are only four types of irrational belief:

1. Demands on oneself, other persons, or life, fate and the universe;
2. 'Awfulising', or 'catastrophising';
3. Low frustration tolerance, or 'I-Can't-Stand-It-Itis';
4. Globally rating the worth of oneself, others, and situations.

Demands

Demands on oneself are expressed as 'I must/should/have to/ought to:

- act competently, and achieve in any activity which is any way significant or important to me;
- behave correctly at all times;
- be approved of and accepted by anybody who matters to me.'

Demands on others are expressed as 'You must:

- act competently and correctly in situations where I say and think you should; people should do as I want (demand) them to.'

Demands on life, fate and the universe are expressed as 'Life, fate and the universe must:
- be fair, especially to me, at all times and according to my prescriptions;
- treat me well, give me a good time, not make demands on me, allow me to get what I want with minimal delay, discomfort, uncertainty and effort;
- give me guarantees, meaning that when I make an effort or sacrifice, I will be rewarded.'

These demands are often expressed as negatives, such as 'Oh no, not again. It shouldn't happen. It's so unfair. After all that effort, I am still not getting the job I have tried so hard to get.'

Awfulising

This means that when things are not good, they are not just somewhat unsatisfactory, they are totally bad. There are no shades of grey, only white or black, the blackest black.

Low Frustration Tolerance (LFT) or I-Can't-Stand-It-Itis

This is usually found lurking around with Awfulising; they are the dynamic duo. I-Can't-Stand-It means not only do I not like the situation, but I cannot bear it. I cannot cope emotionally, and I can't do anything to make things better. This leads to a sense of feeling overwhelmed and hopeless. Awfulising and LFT may be the response to the situation, or to the symptoms of anxiety, or both, and they cause big-time trouble — avoidance. If young Freddie procrastinates over starting an assignment, it may be because he fears doing a bad job, and thinking about it makes him anxious. If he dodges having to read out his work at his tutorial group, it may be because he fears disapproval because of (a) his poor effort or (b) obvious anxiety, and he could not stand that disapproval. (I-Can't- Stand-It-Itis)

Global rating

This can apply to:
- yourself;

- other people; or
- situations and objects.

Global rating leads to the total condemnation, and sometimes the irrational glorification, of yourself or other people. Pop stars, politicians, public figures, and you too, may have many fine attributes in some, or even many, ways. But you, and they, cannot be totally admirable people. Why? Because you are human. It is also the reason for someone with performance anxiety overvaluing the importance of a particular occasion, examination, contest, competition or even a friendly game of bridge.

What is the key to thinking and behaving rationally, avoiding these daft beliefs and philosophies? Have preferences only.

Instead of the 'musts', 'shoulds' and so on, the demands on yourself, others and life, it is far more sensible to have only preferences, no matter how strong. If you want very much to pass an exam, you will work very hard. If you believe that you must pass the exam, you will be anxious, which may paralyse you so that you don't work nearly as hard as you want to.

If things work out badly, or threaten to, instead of telling yourself that it's awful and you can't stand it, you will feel better and handle the situation better if you tell yourself that no matter what the effects are, and how upset you are, you can stand it. This is always true.

Refuse to rate yourself or other people

If you believe it is possible for you to be totally worthless, or that it is possible to objectively and scientifically measure the worth of a human being, you are opening the door to the erosion of your self-regard, and lasting problems with others. If your self-worth is on the line in every contest or examination in which you choose to participate, you are playing for very high stakes indeed. It is a very effective way to create anxiety, even terror.

Many people find it hard to grasp this concept, because it flies in the face of what they have believed all their lives. But when people learn to refuse to rate themselves and other people, it makes it very much easier for them to think rationally in all areas of their lives. These irrational beliefs will be tackled in detail in the next few chapters.

Losing irrational beliefs

Identify your irrational beliefs, assume that they are the cause of your disturbance, demolish them and replace them with rational beliefs. This is the heart of REBT, and central to overcoming performance anxiety.

You may think that if don't believe you must succeed, you will not achieve some important goal, and will consequently be a failure. You may also believe that, robbed of your ambition, you will stop working and striving. Perhaps you can even forget about having any ambitions at all. If this is your thinking, read on.

Losing irrational beliefs never did anyone any harm and it never will. On the contrary, it can only help you feel calmer and happier, and make it easier for you to enjoy what you are doing, while continuing to work hard. Most people who lose their performance anxiety find that as a consequence, they actually perform better.

Let us go back to John, Anne and the others, who helped introduce some different forms of performance anxiety.

John, the concert pianist and full-time perfectionist, makes himself anxious and fearful, and gives himself some nasty symptoms by believing that he must succeed (however he measures success), and that if he fails he is a less worthwhile person. The result is that he has to get everything right all the time, which robs him of much of life's enjoyment and puts a strain on his loved ones.

Anne, the lawyer, is more fortunate than John, in that performance anxiety does not intrude into all of her life. In her career, however, she terrorises herself with the powerful combination of needing success and approval from her legal colleagues. These needs are reinforced by her self-rating tendency in that situation. Also, she overvalues the event and sees a day in court as being a milestone in her life. The truth is that it is only a moment in her life.

Tom, the student, seems to be driven by a devout belief that it is possible for him to achieve, or be granted, a life of success and comfort without his having to do any work or make any other sacrifices to gain it. We have all met people like Tom. It gets worse for him, because his attitudes lead to avoidance and failure, so it becomes easy for Tom to see himself as an ineffectual, weak and worthless person. Self-labelling like that is a potent cause of depression.

Susan, the housewife, has more than a touch of Anne's problem, except that for her it extends throughout most areas of her life. Her principal demon is her dire need for approval.

Gordon, the golfer, practically worships the notion that it is possible to measure the worth of a person, and believes that the yardstick of human worth is how well people perform at some task or other. Of course it is Gordon who decides what tasks matter. He might sound grandiose, but he is quite democratic about it; he beats his chest at times, but in his darker moments he fears he will fail, and will thus be shown to be no better than anybody else, meaning not good enough.

Julie, the student, is on a training program. She is changing the preferences of her loving parents, into the belief that in order to for her to be a good daughter and a good person, she has to please significant people, by succeeding, and that to fail, or not do well, is much more than disappointing and inconvenient. It is a catastrophe. Her parents cannot see the irony in what they are doing, that they are unwittingly doing her a great harm.

Perhaps the descriptions of Julie, Gordon, Anne and the others seem rather extreme and hard to relate to, but it's a fact that there is an element of them (and their strongly held beliefs) in many of us. Never mind that our worth cannot be measured, and that approval and success come with no guarantees of enduring. We go on thinking this way despite the fact that it does us no good, and in fact usually does us plenty of harm. Our little group would have much more comfortable lives, and probably more successful ones, if they could rid themselves of their irrational thinking.

If it is harmful and self-defeating, why do so many people have such a strong tendency to think irrationally?

Why do we continue to fear failure, as if it is dangerous to fail? After all, failing at something does not usually lead to death or mutilation. It simply means only that we did not get an exam pass, a gold medal, a job or some other prize. Conversely, when we succeed, we do not achieve divinity. You have probably noticed that on those occasions when you have competed in a relaxed frame of mind, without an overwhelming need to win, you have felt good, you have enjoyed the game, and you have played or performed well.

RWF treats young doctors who have trouble passing post-graduate examinations because of excessive anxiety, usually about the oral examinations. These exams always come in a group, clustered over two or three days, and candidates must pass them all. Several people have told him how they did badly in a morning exam, and knew that they had blown their chances for that attempt. They could have gone home right then, but they had paid their money and they could not try again for another six or twelve months. So they decided to do the rest of the exams for practice. With nothing to lose, they were calm, and confident in their knowledge of the subject, and almost invariably did well enough to pass. You may have had comparable experiences.

The same applies to you if you find that there is a difference in your level of comfort and/or the quality of your performance in practice or rehearsal compared with performance or competition.

We are all familiar with anxiety, and we often find that the same kind of situation, repeated, makes us anxious again and again. This means we are failing to learn what is causing the anxiety, and what to do about it. We are slow to recognise that our beliefs cause us to think and behave the way we do.

Why don't we learn? Well, we often do, but the process is a slow one.

Most middle-aged people often comment that they have grown not only older, but wiser, than they were in their youth. They say that they have a much better idea now of what does and does not matter in life. They could also add that they have slowly learned to discard their youthful demands, replacing them with wishes and preferences.

When we are in situations that lead us to think ourselves into a state of anxiety, we are not presented with the other possibility, of thinking unanxiously. Further, we tend to focus on the situation and blame that for the way we feel. We erroneously think A causes C, instead of A activating B, which leads to C. In other words, we tend to ignore, or we do not realise, the crucial role that our beliefs play in creating, or doing away with, our anxiety. So, seeking to make ourselves more comfortable, we are more likely to seek ways of changing or avoiding the situation, and less likely to tell ourselves that we can change our thoughts in order to become unafraid.

In addition, we have an innate tendency to think negatively, and are inclined to draw wrong conclusions, and to formulate unhelpful theories about ourselves and the world. RWF was recently told by a medical postgraduate student that he believed he was not the sort of person who could pass exams, thus ignoring the fact that he had passed plenty in his life.

The roles of parents, friends and society

Early in our lives, our parents, family, friends and society generally teach us many things, some good and some much less so, from which we build up a personal philosophy, a set of beliefs that guide our feelings and our actions. We also form our own theories about ourselves, other people and life in general. For example, there is the irrational and self-defeating belief that we must be accepted and/or succeed in order to be worthwhile people. As we grow older we have experiences that activate these beliefs, and even when the beliefs are irrational and get us into trouble, we tend to cling to them as if they are precious gems.

We selectively filter out perceptions that conflict with what we believe, and focus on those bits of information that reinforce it. For instance, if a woman believes that she is unworthy and unlikeable, she will discount the fact that people remember her birthday and show an interest in her progress in school and at university, and that some men are obviously attracted to her. She will emphasise in her mind that sometimes people are distracted when she talks, don't respond as she would wish when she confides in them, or sometimes forget to ring her up. She uses her selective treatment of the evidence to reinforce her belief that she is unlikeable. Does she enjoy holding this negative view of herself? Of course not, but it is easier to cling to a belief, even when it causes pain, than to question it, challenge it, expose its silliness, and replace it with a beneficial belief.

We tend to be mentally lazy. Because of this foolishness, some people manage to ignore inconvenient evidence and retain irrational beliefs for a whole lifetime. Think of elderly politicians and other prominent citizens who with great conviction and no insight make public utterances that are most notable for their ignorance and bigotry. Others lose, but slowly, their irrational beliefs, and develop a more rational and self-enhancing philosophy,

Expanding the REBT model

Psychotherapy aims to speed up the process of learning and changing, and REBT does this efficiently.

The REBT model introduced in the previous chapter, A $\rightarrow$ >B $\rightarrow$ >C, now expands to A $\rightarrow$ > B $\rightarrow$ > C $\rightarrow$ > D $\rightarrow$ > E: Activating event $\rightarrow$ > Beliefs $\rightarrow$ > Consequences $\rightarrow$ > Disputing $\rightarrow$ > Effective new rational beliefs.

1. The As (activating events) need to be identified and clarified. It is not enough, for example, for someone to declare that they are excessively anxious about doing examinations. More detail is needed. Take Julie, the student. In her case the activating events will probably include her entering the exam room, sitting down at the desk and looking at the examination paper. They could also include, in the preceding weeks and months, spontaneous memories of past examinations, momentarily thinking of the exam ahead of her, sitting at her desk and trying to study, hearing friends talk confidently about their exam prospects, and so on.

2. The Cs (consequences) need to be established. They are the guide to the beliefs. Different emotions are associated with different thinking patterns and types of irrational belief. Julie's anxiety tells us she is afraid that something bad will happen to her, that it will be really bad and she will not be able to cope with it. Her depressed mood suggests that she is thinking negatively about herself and/or her life and future. This fits with her expressions of low self-confidence in general.

   If she were angry, her self-talk would reflect different beliefs and have a different pattern. For each emotional C, there is a characteristic pattern of self-talk, reflecting a characteristic set of beliefs. This connection is so strong that once you know the A and the C(s), you pretty accurately deduce what the self-talk is.

3. The Cs lead us to the Bs (beliefs), which we assume are irrational because they give rise to irrational emotional and behavioural consequences (feeling excessively and inappropriately uncomfortable, and acting in self-defeating ways).

4. The irrational beliefs are disputed. This process is done mostly by rigorously challenging the beliefs in all their aspects. Something that will always be found is demands, musts and shoulds. For example, Gordon the golfer would be invited to explain why he absolutely must win at everything, and what would be the implications for him and his life if he did not. Does he turn into a worm on those occasions when he loses?

   This disputing process is not always easy. Do you think someone like Gordon would readily give up his cherished beliefs? Might not his discussion with a therapist seem to him another contest that has to be won? The Gordons of the world who are reading this book may be feeling irritated and combative. If so, they should examine their thoughts, listening for the demands, the shoulds and musts. They have to be there, somewhere.

5. The irrational beliefs need to be replaced with effective rational beliefs. Rational beliefs cannot be taken 'off the peg' and bestowed on someone; the individual has to work them out so that they feel right for them. Rational beliefs are logical, factual, realistic, believable, flexible, not exaggerated or grandiose, and certainly not 'Pollyanna-ish'.

   Rational beliefs are not the same as 'positive affirmations'. With student Tom's record of avoidance and mediocre results, it would be of little use to him to chant 50 times a day 'I am brilliant and bold. I concentrate very well, and I will excel.' Perhaps those statements are true, or potentially so, but why should he believe it when he is struggling to get out of bed? He would be likely to do better if he trained himself to think that the past was regrettable but not too bad, and that he does have the capacity to work and succeed. He would know there are no guarantees, but whatever he does, and whatever happens, he will always be a worthwhile person.

6. REBT exercises and techniques (Chapter 15). What needs to be done now is to bring about the development of good and strong *emotional* insight. This means the person not only

thinks it is right for them to hold a certain rational belief, but feels it, knows it to be true. When this stage is reached, a person can look you in the eye and say they know their worth as a person does not depend on having anyone approve of them, yet they still may be shy, or unable to assert themselves. This is the time for the homework, described in ensuing chapters. It is a fact that the rate of progress is proportional to the amount of time spent doing appropriate homework exercises.

Note: The next chapters will deal with the major irrational beliefs, one by one. Some will apply to you and your particular problems in a very obvious way, and it will be plain that you will need to work on them in order to overcome your difficulties. Some chapters will appear not to apply to you at all. This may truly be the case, or it may just seem that way, initially. Read each one carefully, anyway. If a chapter does not apply to you, you will not be wasting time, and you may learn something useful.

Similarly, the behavioural and coping strategies will be described in detail in ensuing chapters.

Should: Don't get hung up on this word. It's not that you should never think or say 'should', or its equivalents such as 'must', 'have to' and so on. After all, to cross the road safely, you *must* keep your eyes open, and listen for trucks. Here, 'must' is used in a conditional sense, not a demanding one. It is not an ethical or moral issue, but a commonsense, survival one. So it is true that young Johnny must study hard in order to pass his exams, but not to make himself a worthwhile person or to satisfy anyone's wishes.

5 First Catch Your Irrational Beliefs

Our goal is to dispute, challenge and demolish irrational beliefs and personal philosophies that are the basis and the cause of performance anxiety, and to replace them with self-enhancing rational beliefs and philosophies.

But first we must determine, and very clearly, exactly what our irrational ideas are. This is not always easy, but it must be done.

In our day-to-day self-talk, we do not think about our philosophies; rather, we are aware of the thoughts derived from them. So, when I am about to play in the finals of the local tennis club, and I am feeling afraid, I am thinking: 'This will be tough. Jim is in really good form and I don't know what I will do if I lose. I won't be able to face myself tomorrow if I don't win.' I am probably not thinking: 'I absolutely must always succeed at any worthwhile thing that I attempt, and any time that I don't succeed will be evidence that I am a failure as a person.'

My self-talk ('This will be tough ...') is the start of a trail which can lead me to my beliefs and personal philosophies. In this example the A and the C are pretty plain, and so is the B. 'I won't be able to face myself' implies very strongly that I will think less of myself, negatively evaluate myself, should I not win the tennis match. My self-talk could easily be translated into 'If I don't win this match, it will prove I am a failure.'

Because uncovering basic beliefs and philosophies is not always as easy as that, the following exercise is intended to help you develop awareness of your negative self-talk in general, and most particularly negative self-talk associated with experiences of performance anxiety. You need to develop the skills of listening to, analysing and understanding your self-talk; this then leads on to the target irrational beliefs and philosophies. Ultimately, it is these that must be changed.

Developing sensitivity to your self-talk — start keeping a stress diary

Keep a notebook and pen with you at all times. Whenever you feel anxious about a performance challenge, take a couple of minutes as soon as you can. Think back over what happened, and in your stress diary record:

- the activating event — an external event (something that happens) or an image, memory or fantasy;
- the consequences — including:
  (i) any emotion(s) you experienced, and the overall SUDS;
  (ii) physical symptoms, such as breathlessness, or tightness in the chest. Indicate with an * the first symptom that you noticed;
  (iii) any disturbance of mental functioning — whether your mind was racing or slow, confused or detached;
  (iv) what you did, such as pacing, irritable behaviour, avoiding, or procrastinating.
- your self-talk at the time of the incident (not at the time of recording).

Julie's stress diary
Overleaf is an example from the diary of Julie, the high school student.

There are several reasons for keeping a stress diary:
- It will help you become more aware of how your anxiety is sustained by recurrent intrusive negative thoughts and images;
- It will help you become more aware of your self-talk, and this knowledge will in turn lead to the uncovering of your beliefs and personal philosophies;
- It will make you more aware of your Cs, how you respond

emotionally and physiologically, and behaviourally when you become disturbed in a particular context;

- You will learn how your behavioural responses reflect, and are a guide to, your self-talk and emotions; and

- As you become more sensitive to your Cs at low SUDS levels, you can more easily and effectively apply the coping skills described in this book — Rapid Relaxation, Self-Instructional Training and other cognitive interventions.

A What happened	C Emotion(s) Symptom(s) Earliest symptom(s)* What I did	B Self-talk (at the time)
Monday 7.30 Woke up thinking about the exams.	Afraid — Suds 6 + Nausea.* Quickly put it out of my mind.	I don't like studying and I don't like exams. I wish I didn't have to do exams.
10.30 Physics class. I'm not understanding the topic well.	Anxious — Suds 5–6 Irritable. Stomach tight.* Tried hard to concentrate.	I'm no good at this. What if I can't get on top of this subject? What if I can't get into Medicine? I'm as smart as everybody else, so why can't I understand this stuff?
12.30 Talked to Lisa. She's a good student.	Despondent — Suds 5–6 I felt dumb. Sinking feeling in the stomach.* Weak and tired. Silent — couldn't talk.	Lisa is so bright. She'll do well. I'm hopeless. I'm going to fail. What will I do next year?
8 pm Trying to study. Mind racing. Can't concentrate.	Scared — Suds 6 Stomach and chest tight.* Drank hot chocolate.	I hate studying. I'll fail, for sure.

Julie's stress diary

The three major irrational emotions

There are three major irrational negative emotions. Think of them as being like the primary colours. They are:

- anxiety;
- depressed mood (misery), which is not the same as clinical depressive illness;
- anger.

Each irrational emotion has a rational counterpart that is cooler and briefer, and feels appropriate to the circumstances. Rational emotions result from rational self-talk which expresses *preferences* instead of demands. Rational emotions are accompanied by moderate, controllable physical symptoms (or none) and behaviour that helps you achieve your reasonable goals.

Concern is the rational counterpart of anxiety.

Sadness and disappointment are the rational counterparts of depression.

Annoyance is the rational counterpart of anger.

Now let us look at each of these emotions, both irrational and rational, and their self-talk patterns, one at a time.

Characteristic rational and irrational self-talk patterns

1. Anxiety (Irrational)

For anxiety, the irrational self-talk pattern involves:

- predicting that a bad event will happen to oneself or to someone that you care about ('fortune-telling');
- magnifying the ill consequences ('awfulising' or 'catastrophising');
- denying or minimising your ability to cope, emotionally and behaviourally. This is expressed as 'I couldn't stand it.' (low frustration tolerance or LFT)

'I have to read my essay aloud to my class tomorrow.' (statement of fact)

'I'll make a mess of it and look stupid.' (fortune-telling)

'That would be dreadful.' (awfulising)

'I can't bear to think of it.' (I-Can't-Stand-It-Itis or LFT)

Concern (Rational)
The self-talk that leads to concern contains no fortune-telling, awfulising or LFT.

'I have to read my essay aloud to my class tomorrow.' (statement of fact)

'I am not confident that I will do well, because my preparation has been poor.' (realistic assessment)

'Even if it is badly received, there are worse things that could happen.' (realistic assessment).

'I would not like that at all, but it won't kill me.' (I-can-stand-it)

2. Depression (Irrational)
The self-talk that causes depression always contains negative thoughts about:

■ oneself — this usually consists of a global (total) rating of the self, such as calling himself 'hopeless', 'loser' or 'a failure';

■ one's life, one's world, and other people — 'You can't rely on anyone these days.' (= everyone is unreliable);

■ one's future — in terms such as 'hopeless' or 'I'll never succeed' or 'there's no point in trying', which reflects LFT, awfulising and global rating of the situation.

This pattern of negative thinking about your life, your world in relation to other people, and your future, is referred to as Beck's Triad, named after Aaron Beck, the American psychiatrist and cognitive behaviour therapy pioneer. So if someone feels down, glum, flat, unhappy, depressed or miserable, look for one, two or all three of those elements of self-talk.

'I read out my essay in class. It was not a good effort, and no one was impressed.' (statement of fact)

'I'm hopeless.' (global negative self-rating)

'I'll fail the subject and the year. My future looks bleak.' (fortune-telling and awfulising)

Sadness and disappointment (Rational)
These are the natural feelings that occur when a person loses someone or something that they hold important, or they fail to achieve an important goal.

The self-talk that could lead to such feelings focuses not on the self or the person's life, but on the loss. There is no awfulising or global rating.

'I read out my essay in class. It was not a good effort, and no one was impressed.' (statement of fact)

'I wish I had tried harder, and I'd better from now on.' (states a preference — no demands or global self-rating)

'Their response was disappointing, but I'll get over it.' (does not globally, negatively, rate his fellow humans or awfulise about the future)

3. Anger (Irrational)

The target of the self-talk that causes anger is another person, or people, a social institution, or fate. It can be oneself.

'You/he/she/they have done, are doing, or will do something or other, or I believe this to be the case.' (statement of fact)

'You/they should not do it.' (a demand for the other person to comply with a some moral law invoked by the speaker)

'Therefore you/they are no good!' (global negative rating)

Anger is hardly ever rational. However, it is hard to convince people that their anger is not justified, beneficial and sensible. After all, if you believe you have the right to demand how others should behave, surely it follows that you are right when you express this demand, and your indignation and self-righteousness are only fitting.

(RWF: Since I started practising REBT in earnest about 10 years ago, I have found that I become angry much less often and less intensely, and I get over it quicker. What is also interesting to me is that even while I feel angry, I have a sense that it's all pretty silly.)

Annoyance (Rational)

This is the rational counterpart of anger.

'I believe you/she/they have done or are doing something or other.' (statement of fact)

'It is objectionable for one reason or another. I don't like it and I wish you had not, or would not.' (there are no demands or global rating)

So, rational and irrational emotions are different in their effects, and they are also fundamentally different in their self-talk. Irrational emotions are the result of self-talk which contains shoulds and musts, 'awfulising' and global rating. Rational self-talk has none of these, and expresses only preferences. A rational philosophy acknowledges that bad things must and will happen, that life is not perfect and that things will happen which cause distress. It does not demand that people or life's events should be better than they are. Further, a rational philosophy states that rotten behaviour or inferior performance do not equal an inferior person.

The task is to recognise the specific patterns of self-talk that cause you to feel anxious, depressed or angry, and to consciously change your self-talk to a pattern that will help you feel good. When you do this you will not be destroying your ambition. In fact, you will be more likely to succeed, because you will not be driving yourself barmy with irrational demands, 'awfulising', LFT and global rating.

Inference chaining

Inference chaining is the technique that can take you from the start of the self-talk trail to the end, where you will find negative evaluations, irrational evaluations, basic irrational beliefs and personal philosophies. The aim is to challenge, uproot and demolish these disturbing beliefs, and replace them with rational life-enhancing beliefs and philosophies. But first, we must find them.

In inference chaining, you start with the observation or inference, and then by persistently asking questions, and then questioning the answers you get, you follow the trail all the way to the core irrational belief. This should be done on paper, certainly at the start, when you are becoming familiar with it.

To inference-chain, look at each of the statements in your B column. For example, see Julie's diary, page 46. You will probably notice that some are obviously rational and undisturbing, while others are not. As you look at each statement and think about it, note how you feel, pick out the statement that feels most disturbing, and set about querying it.

Persistently ask questions such as:

'If that were true, why would that upset me?'
'If that were true, what would that mean for me?'
'If that were true, what would that mean about me?'
'If that were true, why would that be bad?'
'If that were true, why would that be bad for me?'

'If that were true, just how bad would that be?'

Each inference in the chain is not challenged, but is treated as if it is a fact. At the end of the trail, you can expect to find one or more of the core irrational beliefs (iBs) such as demands, awfulising, LFT or something dire about yourself or your life.

Remember, the type of emotion, as revealed in the C column, gives a strong clue as to the core beliefs, and the self-talk which derives from them. Knowing what the disturbed emotion is, you will set out with a good idea of the sort of iBs that inference chaining will reveal.

Julie's inference chain

Let us look at Julie's examples, her diary entries.

7.30 am Julie's C was anxiety, and in her Bs the most disturbing line of self-talk was 'I wish I didn't have to do exams.' Her inference chaining for this statement might be as follows:

Q. Why is that so?
A. Because I don't like them.
Q. I don't like them. So does this mean they are bad for me?
A. Yes.
Q. If this is true, why are they bad for me?
A. Because I might fail.
Q. If this happens, what would that mean for me?
A. Then I couldn't become a doctor.
Q. If this is true, what would that mean for me?
A. People would see me as a failure.
Q. If this is true, how bad would that be?
A. That would be awful.
Q. Why would it be awful?
A. It would mean that I am a failure. (core irrational belief)

Julie has thus revealed her need for approval, her need to succeed, and her negative global self-rating. She was anxious because she was predicting that something very bad would happen (that she would be shown to be a failure), and was awfulising about it. Her negative self-rating gives a hint that she might be prone to feeling depressed, and this is confirmed by her later entries.

10.30 am Julie's B column contains five questions and statements. In order to work out which is the troublesome one, she thinks about them all, and finds that when she focuses on the question 'Why can't I understand this stuff?' she feels most disturbed. She decides to question it, and seek the underlying core irrational belief.

Q.   Why does that statement disturb me?

A.   Perhaps it means that I am not bright enough.

Q.   If that is true, why is it bad for me?

A.   Perhaps I won't get into medicine.

Q.   Supposing this is true, why does that thought disturb me?

A.   Because I couldn't do the course I have set my heart on.

Q.   If this is true, how bad would that be?

A.   That would be awful.

Q.   Why would it be awful?

A.   It would prove that I am a failure.

Julie was feeling anxious, so she had to be predicting some dire event in her future, and she was. She has again been predicting that she will be proved to be a failure.

12.30 pm Julie says 'I'm going to fail. What will I do next year?'

Q.   Why is that thought disturbing to me?

A.   Perhaps I'll be unemployed or have a menial job, or repeat the year and fail again, and that will the end of my hopes of becoming a doctor.

Q.   If that is true, why would it be so bad for me?

A.   I would never be able to do anything useful or interesting.

Q.   Supposing that is true, why would that be bad?

A.   My life would be boring and pointless.

Q.   Supposing that is true, how bad would that be?

A.   It would be awful.

Julie's questions have led her to discover the belief that for her to fail her exams would mean her future would be no good; she is rating her future as awful (awfulising). This negative thinking about her future causes a depressed mood.

8.00 pm Julie's thought 'I'll fail for sure', is probably the most disturbing one.

Inference-chaining would lead to the same core beliefs revealed at 10.30 am and 12.30 pm. Julie's self-talk has been the type which causes anxiety and depression, and inference-chaining has uncovered the core beliefs from which her self-talk springs.

Gordon's inference chain

Gordon the golfer is different (see Chapter 1) He refers to himself as a 'success' and has a poor opinion of 'losers'. One of his diary entries might read like this.

(A) Activating Event	(C) Consequences	(B) Beliefs
Jones beat me in the play-off for the club championship.	Furious. SUDS 7. Wanted to break my putter. Made an excuse to go home early.	I put a lot into this And I blew it. I'm an idiot. Look at Jones poncing around pretending to be gracious in victory. Damn! I don't want to talk to anyone.

Column C shows anger. This is supported by the angry self-talk in column B. Gordon is angry at both himself and Jones. Column C also shows social withdrawal, which could be caused by anger, depression or anxiety. Gordon can clarify this by mentally going back to the situation, picturing himself not wanting to talk to anyone, and leaving early, and asking himself how he feels at that moment. When he does this, he finds that he is miserable, which reflects his feelings in the situation.

Column B includes global negative rating of himself and Jones. There are no 'shoulds' expressed, but it is pretty obvious that he believes he should have won and Jones should have been less triumphant. The last two sentences, referring to his social withdrawal, do not conflict with his depressed feelings. They could be angry thoughts; he can clarify this by visualising the scene, repeating the two self-talk sentences to himself, and noting whether he feels more depressed or more angry.

Note: People who are frequently irritable, angry and aggressive are very often depressed, with a poor opinion of themselves. They give themselves a bad time, and take it out on everyone around them. People see them as aggressive and hostile, but on the inside they are unhappy. So if you find angry feelings and self-talk in your records, look for the negative self-evaluations which may be there.

Gordon might apply inference-chaining to two of his self-talk statements. The first is 'I put a lot into it, and I blew it.'

Q. Why does that disturb me?
A. Because with that much effort I should have won.
Q. If that is true, why does that thought disturb me?
A. It means I didn't try hard enough.
Q. If that is true, what does that say about me?
A. It means I am lazy and weak.
Q. If that is true, what does that mean?
A. It means that I'm a failure.

The inference-chaining shows that Gordon strives to win in order to not be revealed as a failure. No wonder he became angry at himself when he lost, and depressed later. His statement 'I'm an idiot' fits neatly as the last line of a chain of angry self-talk, and, being a global negative self-rating, it can also cause him to feel depressed.

Self-anger

Fairly often people with performance anxiety become angry with themselves, and later on depressed. The reason for this is clear in their self-talk. Remember the self-talk patterns for anger and depression? In each case there is a negative rating of the entire person, so Gordon's anger involves calling himself an idiot. If he does that often enough, he will come to believe that he really is an idiot, which surely must depress him.

The second statement is 'I don't want to talk to anyone.'

Q. Why would it be bad to talk to someone?
A. Because I feel ashamed.
Q. Why am I ashamed?
A. I didn't try hard enough and they know it.
Q. If that is true, why does it disturb me?
A. They think I'm a loser.

Q. If that is true, why would it be bad?
A. It proves I'm a loser.

There again is global negative self-rating, which is depressing, but he has also revealed a need for approval. This might be a surprising discovery for Gordon and for those around him, as he is often scornful of other's opinions. Now, it appears that he dismisses them because he fears them.

At the end of this exercise you will probably be able to come up with your favourite irrational ideas and philosophies. These are the ideas that are at the heart of your performance anxiety. Now you know your enemy.

6 Disputing — the heart of REBT

We have now reached D (disputing) in the ABCs of Rational-Emotive Behaviour Therapy. Once the irrational beliefs have been accurately identified, the next, essential, task is to attack them. They must be demolished, in preparation for replacing them with new, rational beliefs. REBT disputing is not complex, but it does require a thorough approach.

Because irrational beliefs are usually very well entrenched, it is necessary to vigorously dispute and destroy them in order to replace them with rational ones. Typically, irrational beliefs have been present for a long time, and have been overlearned to the point of achieving an almost holy status. For instance, if you indoctrinate yourself with negative self-statements and distressing images of self-destruction before any kind of performance, several times a day for many years, this amounts to thousands of instances of attaching those predictions, ideas and emotions to the act of auditioning. That is, you condition (teach) yourself to imagine bad feelings and a bad performance whenever you think of an audition. It is unrealistic to hope that simply learning rational beliefs and images will expel the irrational ones. After all, you have to strongly believe in the new rational ideas, not just pay them lip service, and that won't happen if they have to compete against strongly held irrational beliefs for pre-eminence. This is one time in your life when you need to leave no stone unturned. First, the irrational beliefs must be revealed (Chapter 5).

Susan's inference-chaining

You remember Susan, the ultra-nervous, socially anxious wife and mother? Suppose that she had been introduced to a potential new friend, Mary (A — activating event). Later, reflecting on the meeting, Susan recalled that Mary had seemed unimpressed with her. Susan now feels anxious and very miserable (C — consequences).

Her self-talk (B — belief) is:

* 'Mary didn't listen to me.'
* 'She thinks I'm boring.'
* 'She's right. I am boring.'

Susan is feeling unduly upset, so her self-talk (B) must be irrational, and must contain a demand on herself, others and life. There is no demand actually expressed in her self-talk, but there is at least one implied. With inference-chaining, Susan can detect her implicit irrational demands.

Her self-talk is: 'Mary didn't listen to me, so she thinks I'm boring.'

Q. Suppose that is true. Why would it be bad for me?
A. I wanted her to think I was interesting.
Q. If she thinks I am not interesting, why would that be bad?
A. Because I worry about what people think of me.
Q. Why is that so important to me?
A. Because I need other people's approval (this equals 'I should get others' approval').
Q. Supposing I don't get their approval, why would that be bad?
A. If I don't get their approval it would mean that there is something wrong with me.
Q. How is that so?
A. Because whatever they believe about me must be true. If Mary thinks I am boring, I must be boring.

Susan now knows that she believes Mary should feel, and show, approval of her. If she does not get Mary's approval, Susan believes that there must be something very wrong with her, such as being boring.

Her self-talk is now:

First statement: Mary did not listen to me, and she thinks I am boring.

Second statement: I should have been interesting to Mary.

Third statement: Because I was boring to her, I must be boring.

■ The first statement consists of an observation of what Susan believes to be facts ('Mary didn't listen to me'), and the inference she has drawn from that ('She thinks I am boring').

■ The second statement ('I should always be interesting to others, including Mary') is a reflection of Susan's personal philosophy concerning herself and other people: that is, that she needs their approval.

■ The third statement ('Mary thinks I am boring, so I must be boring') is Susan globally rating herself as a bore.
  Each statement has to be examined and disputed.

Comprehensive disputing

Comprehensive disputing is a very thorough process in which all self-talk and every irrational belief that gives rise to self-talk is subjected to a series of challenging questions. These questions ask:

■ What is the evidence to support or to refute the belief?

■ What is the logic that underlies the belief, and does it make sense? Is it internally consistent?

■ Is it practical to believe the statement, and on balance does doing so provide more advantages or disadvantages?

***

Note: Re the origin of an irrational belief, it helps to consider how you learned to think and behave according to your irrational beliefs. Perhaps your parents or others taught you by their words or actions. Perhaps you invented the beliefs and their associated behaviours all by yourself. Remember, whatever the source, it was human, and therefore fallible, and not possessed of Divine Wisdom.

This component of the disputing process, the origin of the belief, is mentioned because it can be highly significant in the development of irrational thinking and behaving. Its content for each irrational belief does not vary much, but nevertheless, we encourage you to bear this aspect in mind as you proceed through the disputing process.

***

At this stage, comprehensive disputing may seem fairly laborious, and perhaps it is. But with practice, as you develop more insight into your thought processes, and more skill, disputing becomes easier, quicker and more automatic.

The following diagram, a pictorial representation of the disputing procedure, summarises comprehensive disputing. It may help you to use this diagram, that is, to draw the boxes when you start disputing. Whether or not you do this, keep it in mind and use it whenever you need to dispute disturbing, irrational beliefs; having a mental picture of the disputing process will make it harder for you to overlook any essential step.

Disputing box (general pattern)

Statement to disputed

	What is the evidence?	Is this logical?	Is this thinking helpful?
Concrete	Box 1(a) Is there any evidence to support this statement of belief? What evidence refutes /undermines it? If there is no evidence, then what is probable?	Box 2(a) Is this belief logical? Does it make sense? Is there a law that says it should be so?	Box 3(a) Will believing this help me to do/get what I want? Consider the costs and benefits.
Generalised	Box 1(b) Ask the same questions as above, but as broadly and generally as possible.	Box 2(b) Must I assume that this belief is valid for me, and for all people, in all situations forever and for all people?	Box 3(b) Will holding other beliefs of this type always help, or will it make it harder for me to do/get what I want?
	New, rational belief:		

Let us explain a couple of terms.

- *Concrete disputing* refers to this occasion, this instance, myself, the other person, these events. In Susan's case, it means the occasion when she met Mary, and Mary's reaction to her.

■ *Generalised (or Abstract) disputing* refers to other instances of the same kind of thing, involving people other than Mary. So the disputing process progresses from what Mary thinks about how boring Susan is, to what anybody thinks about any aspect of Susan, to anybody's opinion about any aspect of anybody else. Susan's example will illustrate this, as it is essential to make disputing as broad, general and philosophical as possible. To limit disputing to the specifics of one incident will do very little to help you with other similar experiences.

Susan's first statement: 'Mary didn't listen to me and she thinks I'm boring.'
Box 1(a) What is the evidence? — concrete
Is there any evidence that Mary didn't listen to me, and that she thinks I am a bore? Was she obviously enthralled by anyone's conversation? No. She gave me no clear indication that she thought me dull, and I can't read her mind.

Box 1(b) What is the evidence? — generalised
Do people generally give the impression that I bore them? Do they make feeble excuses to get away from me at social functions, and cross the road to avoid my company? No.

Boxes 2(a) and 2(b)
Questioning the logic doesn't apply when disputing a statement of fact.

Boxes 3(a) and 3(b)
The costs and benefits are relevant. A belief that she bores people will make it harder for Susan to feel good, and to converse interestingly.

Susan's second statement — 'I should have been interesting to Mary.'
Box 1(a) Where is the evidence? — concrete
Susan asks 'Where is the evidence that I should be interesting to Mary?' Night should follow day, and the evidence is that it always does. If I should be interesting to Mary, it has to happen. Did it happen? I don't know. Therefore there is no evidence that I should be interesting to Mary.

Box 1(b) Where is the evidence? — generalised
Using the same reasoning, is there any evidence that I must be
interesting to anybody at all, or that anybody on Earth must
always be interesting to everybody they talk to? If there is such a
law, there should be evidence.

Box 2(a) Is this thinking logical? — concrete
Susan asks 'Why should I have been interesting to Mary? Is there
a law that says I must? Where is it written that she must find me
interesting? Is it logical to insist that simply because I want to be
interesting to her, I must be? Does it make sense to insist that I gain
her interest?' Susan concludes that there is no such law, and that
it is nonsense to believe that she has to be interesting to Mary.

Susan could stop here but she has a much bigger problem — a
general need for approval. So she proceeds to Box 2(b), where she
can practise broader (generalised) disputing of her need to have
everybody think she is interesting. She should do this not only
because her social anxiety is a general problem for her, but
because if she does dispute in a general way, she will achieve an
effect not limited to a single situation.

Box 2(b) Is this thinking logical? — generalised
Susan now asks, 'Is there a law of the universe that says
everybody on this Earth must show an interest in me, or approve
of any of my qualities, or think anything about me at all? No
matter what I want people to do, such as like me, does it make
sense to think that this means that they must do just that?'
Obviously, the answer is no. At this point Susan is attacking her
demand that she be approved of, not only by Mary, but by
anybody else. She has acknowledged that it is reasonable to want
people to approve of her, but she challenges the belief that this
want confirms upon her the power to insist that anybody must
do what she wants them to do.

More generally, she asks the same kind of questions about
whether it is logical, whether there are laws of the universe that
say anyone must give approval, or do anything at all just because
another person wants them to. Logical disputing, by attacking
the sense of irrational beliefs, is an essential disputing technique,
but Susan must press on.

Box 3(a) Is this thinking practical? — concrete

Susan can ask herself how she would like to feel and act when she meets Mary; she will probably prefer to feel calm, appear relaxed, and converse freely and 'interestingly'. She then asks 'If I go on believing that Mary must approve of me and show interest in me, will that help me to feel relaxed and converse interestingly?' Of course it would be no help; in fact it would hinder her.

Box 3(b) Is this thinking practical? — generalised

Susan asks herself the same question, applying it to meeting people in general, and comes up with the same answer. She can ask, 'If I believe that everyone must approve of me and see me as an interesting person, will that make it easier or harder to relax with them and converse interestingly with them (which is what I want)?' Of course she will decide she'd be better off without the belief that everybody must approve of her.

At this point Susan can replace her irrational belief with a statement such as 'It would be nice if Mary liked me, but I don't know what she thought of me. If she was unimpressed, that's disappointing, but there's no law that says that she or anybody else on this Earth must think well of me.' She is still able to want to be liked and approved of, and to be disappointed if she does not impress someone she likes. What Susan is getting rid of is her belief that if she wants to be liked and approved of it *must* happen.

Susan's third statement — 'If Mary thinks I'm boring, then I am boring.'

Box 1(a) What is the evidence? — concrete

Susan asks 'Where is the evidence that any of my qualities have changed because of what Mary thinks about me? Mostly, I don't know what she thinks, but I remember one occasion when she said I looked worried, and she was wrong — I had indigestion.'

Box 1(b) Where is the evidence? — generalised

Susan asks 'Is there any evidence that I have ever been changed by what someone might think of me, or that anyone ever turns into something or someone different, or that they are transformed in any way, because of what someone else thinks about them? Susan can see that there is no evidence to support a belief that anyone's opinion changes anyone else.

Box 2(a) Is this thinking logical? — concrete
Susan asks 'Is it logical to think that I am a boring person simply because Mary thinks I am, that her opinion of me constructs the reality of what I am? Her opinion is only an opinion, and if she changes it, does that mean I must change in order for the reality of me to match her opinion?' She will conclude that Mary's opinion of her is nothing more than that — an opinion.

Box 2(b) Is this thinking logical? — generalised
Susan now asks generally, 'If Mary thinks I'm a hippopotamus, must I look for some nice mud to wallow in? Do I believe that Mary is a god-like creature, whose opinion creates everybody's reality? That is, does everybody else become whatever Mary thinks they are? Does my opinion of somebody mean that they are exactly what I think they are? Does anybody's opinion of me or anybody else mean that I or the other people are exactly what that opinion says they are? Can an opinion, anybody's opinion, about anything at all, be anything more than an opinion?' The answers are no, no, no, no, no and no.

Box 3(a) Is it practical to think this way? — concrete and Box 3(b) Is it practical to think this way — generalised
The questions and answers are similar to the practical disputing of Susan's second statement, 'I should have been interesting to Mary.'

Susan's new rational belief
Susan's rational statement could now be: 'I would have liked Mary to think well of me, and there is no evidence that she didn't. What we think of each other does matter, and I would like her to like me, but she does not have to. I prefer to have people approve of me, so it is disappointing when they don't. But whatever they think of me is never anything more than an opinion. I am what I am, and that's that.'

That is how you will, at least initially, dispute the irrational beliefs that cause your performance anxiety. **It is essential to be thorough.** Do it in writing at first. Eventually, you will be able to dispute 'on your feet', automatically and naturally. But until then, writing is essential if you want to get rid of your performance anxiety. Unfortunately, it is not as easy as swallowing a pill, or just reading a book. You have to work reasonably hard at times, but surely that is better than tormenting yourself with performance anxiety. So get out your disputing box and see your iBs for what they are — to put it bluntly, destructive bits of nonsense.

At this stage, disputing probably appears finickity and tedious. Unfortunately, that's how it often is when you are learning a new skill. It gets easier with practice, and you will find that after a while (not now!) your disputing will look more like this:

1. I bored Mary.
2. I should get Mary's approval, and if she thinks I am boring then I am.

Boxes 1(a) What is the evidence? — concrete
'Is there any evidence that I bored Mary, or that I did not bore her? If there is no evidence of boredom or non-boredom, what is likely?'
Answer: She appeared happy to talk to me, and did not give any of the usual signals of being bored.

Box 1(b) What is the evidence? — generalised
'If I must get Mary's approval now, then I always must — is there evidence that this happens?'
Answer: No.
'Do I absolutely always get everybody's approval?'
Answer: No. Then there can't be a universal law about it. Is there any evidence that I am created by what Mary or anyone else thinks of me?
Answer: Absolutely not.

Box 2(a) Is this thinking logical? — concrete
'Does it make sense that I must get Mary's approval and that if she thinks I'm boring, I am? Is there any law that says that I must get her to approve of me in order for me not to be a boring person?'
Answer: This is plainly nonsense.

Box 2(b) Is this thinking logical? — generalised
'Does it make sense, and is it logical, that I must have anyone's approval, and that whatever they think of me must be the truth? Is there a law that says I must earn people's approval, and that if I don't, I turn into a cockroach?'
Answer: Obviously there is no such law.

Box 3(a) Is this thinking practical? — concrete
'When I meet Mary, I would like to make a good impression, so it would be good for me to be relaxed, and to concentrate on the conversation. Will it help me to tell myself that I have to have her approval and that if she thinks I am a bore, then I am one?'
Answer: No, of course not.'

Box 3(b) Is this thinking practical? — generalised
'When I meet people, I would like them to think well of me, which they are more likely to do if I stay relaxed and keep my mind on the conversation instead of worrying about myself. Would it help me if I believe that they will probably accept me, and that whatever they think of me is only an opinion so they don't have to like me?'
Answer: Yes, obviously.

Eventually, Susan's disputing will look something like this: 'Did Mary give any sign that she was bored by me? No, so she probably wasn't bored. Do I need anyone's good opinion of me in order for me to be a worthwhile person? No. So I probably did interest her, but if I didn't, that's no great problem.'

As you can see, this brief method, which you will use after some practice with the basic method, is a simpler and more straightforward route to the same goal.

The step beyond this is not to have any irrational beliefs to dispute. It usually takes quite a few months, and a lot of experience at disputing before that point is reached.

7 I must act competently and correctly at all times

Once I thought I made a mistake — but I was wrong.
(car sticker)

The belief that you must act competently and correctly at all times is the most common, and usually the most potent, of the irrational beliefs in performance anxiety.

To wish to do well, succeed or win is natural, sensible and logical. It is also helpful, in that it makes no sense to try a new venture, say, entering a competition, signing up for computer training or a writing course, if you are totally indifferent to the outcome. You might as well not bother, and save your time and effort. However, because you are human, you can be absolutely certain that you will make mistakes, and lots of them, in every conceivable situation. That's the way it has to be.

Disputing

The evidence

You might ask yourself, 'Must I always perform well, with no exceptions, half-measures or shades of grey?' Such a demand on oneself would have the force of a law of nature.

You might ask, 'Have I absolutely always, with no exceptions at all, acted competently, in every moment of my life?' This is clearly impossible, so you tell yourself 'As I break an unbreak-able law every day, it obviously cannot exist.' Ask yourself, 'Is there evidence to support a law that says I must make mistakes and act incompetently quite a bit of the time?' Yes. You bet. Ask 'Is there any evidence that anyone at all always achieves exactly as they want to? No. Is there evidence to the contrary?' Plenty of it.

The logic

First, is it logical, does it make sense, to claim that because you want to succeed, you must? In a given situation, say sitting for an examination, you naturally want to succeed, but does this mean you must? Is there a rule, a law, a divine command? Is it inscribed on tablets of gold in heaven?

Other people will say there's no law that says you must pass the examination. Are they right, or are you right just because you believe it and say so? If you insist you are right, are you claiming special knowledge and wisdom? Surely you can convince other people. Find someone who will listen, or take a few minutes to do this in your head, or (much better) in writing. Produce all the arguments you can think of. Let's suppose you couldn't produce a good supporting argument. That's not your fault — it's because there is no supporting argument. Now you could proceed to beat yourself up for having continued to believe in the irrational demand on yourself to always perform excellently. Before you start the auto-pugilism, stop and ask yourself if the tablets of gold mention anything about your not being allowed to have an erroneous belief, or several.

Here's an interesting little paradox. By failing at this task of producing winning arguments, you are succeeding — you are exposing the fact that your belief is unsupportable.

If it is true that you must always perform well and get things right, does the same law apply to others, and do they know about it? If they do, they obviously forget it a lot of the time. Humans act inefficiently, foolishly and even unethically, very often; they are programmed to (that is, they must). Well then, is there is a special rule for you? There are six billion people on this planet and you are superior to all the rest of us? Of course you wouldn't make such a vainglorious claim. Do you then have a one-in-six-billion rule because you are worse than the rest of us? If either of the above applies to you, this book is not for you, because you don't need it, or you are beyond help (you aren't). You're not the King of the World, nor the lowliest microbe, so let us press on.

Note: It is worth mentioning here that we find humour and exaggeration often useful for helping patients through this therapy. It can help them see their irrational beliefs in a new light, without making fun of their predicament.

So we don't for a moment accuse you of having a swollen head. But consider whether you put your performance demands on other people. Perhaps you do — some high-performance demanders are democratic about it, and apply the same standards to everyone else as to themselves. Seems fair, doesn't it? It is, if everyone else agrees to conform to your high standards. If they haven't, or if they don't even know about how well they have to perform, it's a bit rough, isn't it? Or do you tell yourself that you must do well, or succeed at every worthwhile thing you attempt, while excusing everyone else? Nice of you to be kind to others, but why give only yourself a bad time? Have you committed some hideous crime that you have to spend the rest of your life atoning for? If that is not the explanation, then what is?

The usual reason that people give for their perfectionistic self-demands is that they relate their intrinsic worth as a person to how well they do something or other, or just about everything. As you know by now, this sounds something like 'I must do well in the exams/get that promotion at work/impress my audience/ and so on, because if I don't I'm a failure.'

If you must succeed at one particular endeavour, say doing well in examinations, is that enough, or do you have to do well, or win, in everything? Some people are generalists like Gordon. If you are restrictive, why do you pick on one out of so many of life's activities and declare it to be the one you must do well in? Who says that playing the violin, sprinting or getting a promotion is the one thing that must be done excellently? If you do, how do you know that you are right and that those people who make demands on themselves to succeed in a different activity are wrong? You can't all be right, so perhaps no one is right. Yes, that's it. There is no must/should/have-to rule for anyone at all.

I, Eversley Farnbach (EMF), was once taken to task about this irrational belief by a professional violinist, who was irritated to hear her belief about the importance of performance perfection questioned. She told me that she believed that as a professional orchestra member, the consequences of not meeting a certain standard of performance could be her dismissal. Surely, she said, she must play very well (perfectly/excellently) at all times, practising for hours every day. But she was wrong to demand the impossible from herself. Furthermore, if she believed that she must perform perfectly and excellently, always, to keep her job, would this thinking help her to perform calmly and competently? No. Perhaps she would make an excellent (and calm) violin teacher. Even if she couldn't succeed as a violinist, she could always make a complete career change and do something else. That would be a hassle, but would it be a horror? No. It could even be a relief. (I did it.)

Sometimes They-Who-Must-Succeed change their minds about all sorts of things, including what things they must do well at. With the passion comes — or goes — the self-demands. But if it is true that They-Who-Must-Succeed must succeed when they have the passion, how can it not be true at other times?

We are all capable of thinking rationally and irrationally at the same time, on the same topic. The result is: 'It is important for me to do well in this audition, and I really want to very much ... so I must.' This is not so much infantile thinking as being seduced away from rational into irrational thinking by the importance of the challenge.

Preferences, wishes and desires, no matter how strong they are, are not absolute. They leave the door open for compromise and compassion.

Is there any logic in believing that you must succeed? The possible benefit is that it may encourage you to get moving, to try harder and to hang in when things aren't going well. But it may do the opposite, causing inhibition, distraction, disappointment and giving up too easily. It certainly is a giant step on the path to anxiety. This is because of the absolute nature of demands.

A tightrope walker crossing over Niagara Falls must be totally successful. Nothing less will do. This is fine for him, but how do you apply it to examinations, conditions, performances, relationships, making love or anything else. How on earth do you measure success? It is often subjective, and what looks like 100 per cent can sometimes be done better.

There is another problem. You might, this time, do as well as you believe you must. But this won't allow you to rest. There will be the next time, and the time after that. Even if you perform supremely well now, you know it's not possible for you to always do as well as that, without exception, for as long as you live.

Try telling yourself that to succeed might be very good, enjoyable and beneficial; you will try very hard to make it happen, but it doesn't have to work out the way you want it to.

The practical effects

Now consider the effects on you of your beliefs and self-talk. Does it, on balance, do you more good or more harm, to believe that you must succeed at achieving a goal? Will it help you reach this goal, or hinder you? What is the cost–benefit ratio? Consider the following arguments.

If you believe you must succeed at something or other, you have no options. If you believe you must win, no other outcome is conceivable. But the result of thinking this way is confusion and fear — hardly emotions to help you achieve the success required.

Think of the Yerkes-Dodson Relationship. (Fig 2.1) Fear pushes you over the top into the impaired-performance zone. Preferences and wishes take you only up the ascending limb of the arc, where your arousal is appropriate (it feels right) and productive (see Chapter 2).

The cost–benefit ratio (see Chapter 15) of hanging onto 'shoulds', 'musts' and 'have-tos' is so bad, you could class it as a really rotten deal.

The origin of irrational beliefs

Although 'The origin of the irrational belief' is only briefly referred to during the disputing process described in Chapter 6, it can be of particular relevence to some, if not all your irrational thinking, and useful to keep in mind as you dispute your irrational beliefs.

Remember that wherever your irrational beliefs came from, what matters now is that you challenge the authenticity of your source of wisdom. As your source was almost certainly not divine, whoever convinced you to subscribe to your iBs was most assuredly mortal, and therefore fallible. Take the following case study as an example of this.

Case study

Sally, 38, unhappy about her serial monogamy, and convinced she could never succeed in forming a happy and enduring relationship with a man, had been taught as a teenager, by her mother, that this would be her lot in life. When I asked her about her mother's credentials as an authority, she laughed, then told me that her informant had three failed marriages — hardly qualifying her to give advice about meaningful, long-term relationships.

Here is the strange part. Sally is an intelligent woman. Why did she disregard that golden insight for so many years, waiting for someone else to lead her to the obvious? We all have our nonsensical beliefs about ourselves and other people, life and everything else, and we go for years without questioning them. Some of them are harmful. Often, when we are invited to question them, their silliness is almost instantly apparent.

Disputing summary

If you believe that you absolutely must do well, every time you perform, dispute this belief.

1. *What is the evidence? Does it support or oppose the belief? What are the facts of your success so far?*
   My past experience certainly does not provide evidence to support this belief.

2. *Is this belief logical?*
   ▪ Does it make sense to believe that you, a mere mortal, must always succeed whenever you try something that matters to you?
   ▪ Does it make sense to say that because you want something to happen, it must happen?
   ▪ If there is a rule that says that you must always succeed, where does this rule come from? Did the Almighty whisper it in your ear? Does this rule apply to everyone else, all six billion of us?
   ▪ If it does, then does it apply to everyone, and does that mean that we must all do very well at all things, or come first all the time? Or if the rule applies to only you, can you think of a good reason why this should be so?
   ▪ Perhaps there is no such rule. Of course there isn't.

3. *Is it practical to hold this belief? Will holding this belief help get you what you want?*
   You could tell yourself that you absolutely must succeed according to your elevated standards on a given occasion, or tell yourself that you would like to succeed, perhaps even like to very much indeed, that the event is important and that it matters a lot to you.
   ▪ Which belief do you think would allow you to feel comfortably and agreeably aroused to do the best you can? The answer is clear.

Read the following rational statement. Adapt it to your own circumstances and set about learning and living its principles.

New, rational belief

'Success beats failing any day, and for very obvious reasons, I would always prefer to do well at anything that matters to me, and I will try to make this happen. Not to do well at something can be disappointing, inconvenient and disadvantageous, but there is no law that says it must not happen to me, or to anyone. Indeed, because I am human and therefore fallible, I must do things in a mediocre way, and sometimes badly. At times I will not even manage to make a good effort; this also must happen. Meanwhile, I will work hard to do as well as I can as often as I can.'

8 I must be approved of and accepted by everybody

This chapter is about the fear of negative evaluation, the basis of the need for approval and acceptance. Some common terms for negative evaluation are non-acceptance, rejection and disapproval. We will be using these terms interchangeably.

RWF: 'Even people I don't like have to approve of me.' When you have been in psychiatric practice for 30 years, you think you've heard it all; but this statement from Jane, a patient, really pinned my ears back. But she is not alone. From time to time when I quote her words to other patients I hear, 'It's exactly the same for me.' The effect such a nonsensical belief can have on a person's life can devastating; approval-needing, such as Jane's, is the basis of the common psychological disorder, social phobia (Chapter 17). Many of us feel the same need; it may be to a lesser degree, but it is still strong enough for it to cause embarrassment, non-assertive behaviour, excessive desire to please, and, in some people, performance anxiety.

What is wrong with needing approval and acceptance?

Elite sportspeople are more likely to be driven by the need to succeed (fear of failure). Students and amateurs tend to suffer more from the need for approval. However, performers at any level of achievement can be afflicted by any irrational belief, or many, with much overlapping.

What is wrong with needing approval and acceptance? After all, we depend on our family, friends and associates for different things, so doesn't this mean that we need each other's approval? Not really. In primitive societies, being accepted by the tribe was necessary for survival; get enough disapproval and you're out in the snow, the desert or the jungle, all alone. But things have changed for most of us, and such dire consequences of rejection are now rare.

Disapproval is unpleasant, but is that alone bad enough to cause anything more than concern and disappointment? Something else must be happening if the prospect or fact of disapproval is so disturbing that it leads to fear and avoidance. Put your money on 'awfulising', low frustration tolerance (LFT) or global rating (the belief that disapproval proves you to be inferior).

So, the thing that makes rejection bad to the rejectee is that it is seen as a true reflection of the tragic victim's worth as a person. 'If they think I'm stupid/boring/a bad musician, that is what I must be.' Therefore, 'I must be approved of, or I will suffer a fate worse than death — personal worthlessness.'

'I must be approved of' keeps bad company, but deserves to be attacked in its own right. Remember 'I must be approved of' is a statement of a demand, an absolute. No half-measures will be allowed. However, a wish or a preference can often be integrated with an absolute: 'It will be good if my efforts impress people, so I hope to please them. Actually, I must please them.' This is a sneaky trick we play on ourselves; the preference is a Trojan horse distracts and disarms us, and enables the demand to do its dirty work.

Disputing

The evidence

If you ask 'What is the evidence for or against the belief that I must be approved of and accepted by everybody?' you won't find any. All the evidence in the world, about your being revered or loathed by multitudes, can never prove that you must, or must not, gain approval. If you must be accepted, it must happen. But has your life provided evidence that your approval-needing rule is invariably obeyed? If not, there is no rule. It takes only one penguin to disprove the idea that all birds must fly.

The logic

Ask yourself, is the belief that one must always be approved of and accepted by everybody logical? It sounds like a law of the universe, but is it one? Where did this law come from? Does everybody else know about it? If they do know of it, they surely can talk about it to you.

If the rule exists, it must exist for everybody. That is, we assume that you don't consider yourself to be so superior to everybody else that only you deserve to have universal approval, or so inferior to everyone that you must have universal approval in order to justify your fitness to live. That all sounds a bit far-fetched, so if you are just a normal sort of person, the rule that applies to you must apply to everyone else on the planet. This means that everybody must get total approval from everyone else, and everyone else must give approval whenever it is possible to do so. Now we are all living in a lovely warm bath of absolute approval, acceptance and love.

Perhaps there is no such rule, and everyone has the right to approve or disapprove of what you do or what anyone else does. Think about it like this for a moment. By demanding that you be approved of, you are denying others their free will, and are thus assuming divine status for yourself, while knowing that other people really can do what they like. This thinking is internally inconsistent. Can you think of any way to make it consistent? We can't.

If others approve of your efforts today, and perhaps this means you are a worthwhile person, then what if they disapprove tomorrow or the next day? Continual approval can never be guaranteed, which means that needing acceptance and approval makes you vulnerable. It would be better to merely prefer to be accepted, and to truly believe that disapproval, while undesirable and disappointing, is not itself harmful.

If some approve, some disapprove and some are undecided about your performance, what, if anything, does this say about you? Did you ever hear of anyone who was universally acclaimed for anything at all, whether it was for being among the elite of their profession or fields of study, or in the arts, sports, or humanitarian activities? In these and other areas, the excellence of performance is usually decided, not by one person, but by a panel of judges or examiners. If the judges were not human, with free will and the right to their own opinions, then only one would be needed. This applies in the conferring of Nobel prizes, awards in the television and film industries, Olympic sports, oral examinations and international music competitions, for example.

This brings us to the real point. Whatever anyone thinks of you or what you do can never be anything more than an opinion. Even at the highest reaches of science and technology, where you might expect that scientific principles would be all that matters there are still plenty of instances where international experts agree to disagree, not because of hard facts, but because of their interpretations of them. This being the case, how can it possibly be reasonable for you to expect that every person in the audience is going to thoroughly approve of your performance (and you) when you make a speech, or give an exhibition of tap-dancing?

Approval and your worth as a person

Ask yourself if it makes any sense at all to relate your worth as a person to whether somebody approves or disapproves of something that you do. Does it make any difference if it is one person or many, whether the people involved are humble or noble, or what it is that you are doing, that are to pass judgement on? You are infinitely more complex than one or two of your deeds, so even if it were possible to rate your worth as a person (and it is not), to do so on the basis of any one activity is obviously ridiculous. This is even more the case when you consider that the quality of your performance must change from time to time, and so then will people's opinions of it; yet all the time you remain the same person. You are not what others think you are, any more than you are what you do.

Approval and the quality of your life

To have approval of what we do is obviously good, because there are indisputable benefits that come from having family, friends, associates and audiences think well of us. There are obvious drawbacks to having others think badly of what we do, particularly if we are in a competition or examination, or giving a public speech or performance. However, time heals most wounds (because it enables our thinking to evolve and become more rational), and after a week or a month or so, the event would probably not seem as bad as it had at the time. The fact that you are alive and presumably sane, and your health is relatively unimpaired, indicates that you stood even a fruit-pelting occasion, and may perform another day.

If you are in the habit of telling yourself that it would be awful, and you could not stand it if your efforts or your performance were not well regarded, then think again, and tell yourself that disapproval is unpleasant and perhaps inconvenient, but it could never be anything worse than that. (See Chapter 11 concerning Awfulising and Low Frustration Tolerance.)

The practical effects

Ask yourself whether, in a particular instance, it would be in your interests, or against them, for you to believe that people must like or approve of what you do. Try doing that now. Think of yourself about to meet an examination panel, or start a performance or a speech, write a section of a book, ask someone out on a date, give a dinner party, or whatever else you can think of.

While thinking of it, tell yourself that you must, absolutely must have the relevant people think well of what you do. Add, if you wish, the belief that if they disapprove, it means that you are less worthwhile, and it would be awful and that you could not stand it. Notice how anxious you feel. Then tell yourself instead that you would like to impress the other person(s), and there are obvious advantages in doing so, but if you don't, you don't, and that is all there is to it. Notice how different you feel.

The point here is that believing your efforts must be approved of is likely to make you anxious, and to lessen your focus and concentration. The result is that you will probably feel uncomfortable, and your performance will suffer. This hardly fits with your reasonable desire to live a long and happy life.

At a more abstract level, ask yourself the same questions in relation to any activity of yours.

Ask yourself what effect it would have on anybody's comfort

and performance for them to believe that they absolutely must be approved of for whatever they do. The answers will always be the same.

Disputing summary

If you believe that you must always be accepted and approved of by significant people, and that you must not be disapproved of rejected by them, dispute this belief.

1. What is the evidence for or against the belief?
- Does any evidence support the view that you must have approval and acceptance whenever you want it?
- Have you always had complete acceptance and approval when you wanted it, as certainly as night follows day?
- Is it certain that you always will? With no exceptions?

We don't know the answer, but we do know it is most unlikely that you have always had 100 per cent approval from people when you commanded yourself to get it. If you have, you are so lovable you can stop worrying about anything right now.

2. Is the belief logical?
- Does it make sense to demand that you always be approved of? You might desire it greatly, but does this mean that it has to happen?
- When you disapprove of someone, you don't expect them to shrivel up and die, and they don't. You accept it as one of life's inevitabilities that the disapproved-of-person doesn't have to impress you favourably. It cuts both ways.
- As it is impossible for anyone to be universally liked, how smart is it for any individual to insist that they achieve what no human can? It's impossible, because there would always be someone who would despise you for your massive popularity. Of course you don't believe any of that. There is no such law.

3. Is it practical to hold this belief? That is, does thinking this way make it easier or harder for you to achieve your goals?
- You can:
  - (a) want, prefer, even at times intensely desire, to be approved of and accepted, or

(b) you may demand that you gain approval.

Which will help you to be calm, and which will make you fearful? Take your pick. The answer is clear.

Read the following rational statement, and adapt it to your circumstances. Set about learning its principles, and living them.

New rational belief

When people accept me, approve of me, like me and love me, it is pleasant, and it can provide me with practical benefits. But what anyone thinks of me, for any reason at all, can never be anything more than an opinion. As much as I want to be liked, I can never <u>need</u> it. To be disapproved of, while it may be disappointing or unpleasant, can never mean anything about me, and can never hurt me.

9 Everyone must act competently and correctly

One way of upsetting ourselves is to put expectations on other people to behave as we believe they should, and to not accept it when they act upon their belief that they have a right to determine their own behaviour. The irrational belief is that if we would like other people to behave in certain ways, then they must.

Let us consider this belief, with some consideration of how it might apply in performance anxiety.

How does this apply to me?

'People (this includes you and anyone else I nominate) should always act competently, intelligently, sensibly and correctly. Behaving correctly includes acting with care, responsibility, co-operation, compassion, honesty and, above all, with complete awareness of, and respect for, what I deem to be right and proper behaviour.'

'People should also be appreciative of my efforts, and they themselves should work hard. They should not collect rewards to which they are not entitled. So if they don't perform better than I do, then they must not achieve success or obtain rewards greater than mine.'

Most of us are inclined to have views, sometimes strong, about how other people should behave. Holding these views, and, in particular, expressing them, is the cause of much personal distress and interpersonal conflict. It may seem to you that this has little relevance to you, if you have performance anxiety. You may be right, but we suggest you read on.

Do any of the following apply to you?

- Feeling envy, resentment or hostility towards a rival;
- Being excessively critical of other people and their performances;
- Hating, for example, your boss or teacher or coach for their inefficiency, incompetence, lack of consideration or anything else;
- If you are a teacher, becoming angry at a slow pupil;
- Feeling angry or hurt because you are not appreciated;
- When you are let down by someone whose cooperation you were depending on, you are miserable, probably thinking that others should always do as you wish.

Disputing

The evidence

Is there any evidence to support your belief that other people, nominated by you, must always behave competently and ethically? Other people, breathtakingly wilful, have let you down again and again. There is plenty of evidence to support that, isn't there? No? Pity.

The logic

Who says that people should always behave well and competently? Whose rule is this? Did you get it from God? Is it your law? If it is, then why haven't the rest of us heard about it so that we can always do the right thing?

Of course there is no such law. There are only laws of nature, such as the sun rising and setting each day. With laws of nature, there is certainty. The laws that humans make are different. How easy it would be if simply by promulgating democratically determined laws, we could achieve universal compliance. However, people do break them, and that's why we have law enforcement.

So, inconveniently, things don't happen just because we want them to, and other people:

(a) usually don't know about the laws we dream up for them; and

(b) feel free to break them whenever they want to anyway.

The fact is, humans are fallible, and because of this they have misunderstandings, and make foolish errors and stupid mistakes. They do things that are illogical, wrong-headed and unethical. Of course, the less often these things happen, and the less severe the mistakes are, the better it is for all of us. But stupid and wrong things will be done, by absolutely everybody.

Inconveniently for us, however, we are unable to choose who will misbehave, when they will, what they will do, or whether or not we will be the victim. It has always been this way, and always will be. That is how it should be. There is no point in hoping otherwise.

We are all different, so we all have different requirements regarding how we would like people to behave. So who is right? Everybody is right when it is a matter of their personal prefer-ences. When anybody says that what they prefer is a need, and that others must comply with that need, they are logically wrong, apart from causing irritation and resentment.

You have surely been in the company of someone who is angrily ranting about how someone else should have done something or other. Perhaps you thought 'This is a bit over the top. I can see why he is frustrated, but he's overreacting. People do make mistakes.' In that instance, you were probably quite right and the ranter was wrong. Have you ever been the ranter?

Most of us accept in theory the fact of human fallibility, that people must commit errors, but we often forget this when we are affected by what people do, or when we self-indulgently feel like picking on someone. In this latter case, by demanding that others exhibit levels of competence and goodness that we can't aspire to ourselves, it enables us to feel better about ourselves. This thinking is very common, but not at all rational.

The practical effects

Most of us have been on the receiving end of the 'You must behave as I think you should' belief, and have experienced its adverse effects. If you accept the demander's requirements that you behave in a certain way, for example, or that you perform excellently in the arts, work, or study, you may experience anxiety and resentment, and finally, lose focus on the real task.

Outside the performance area, this belief is a potent contributor to marital conflict; much hostility between marriage partners is caused by each person's refusing to accept the inevitable imperfections of their partner. Nobody claims to be perfect, yet many people pretend that they deserve a perfect spouse.

To accept intellectually and emotionally that others must make mistakes will lead to nothing more severe than mild frustration, annoyance or disappointment, and never to any destructive emotional reactions. It is not logical to say that you accept that everyone is fallible, and mistakes must happen, and then to try to pick and choose which mistakes are acceptable.

Disputing summary

If you spend a significant amount of time suffering the discomfort of feeling hurt, resentful or angry because others don't act the way you think they should, question your beliefs. To insist that others should act competently and correctly at all times is irrational and self-harmful, so you had better dispute it.

1. *What is the evidence? Does it support or oppose the belief?*
- The amoeba breeds by splitting in two. It does so because it must. No one has ever observed any deviation from this amoeba reproduction pattern. This is what is meant by 'must' or 'have to'.
- There is abundant evidence that humans are programmed to act the way they do — incompetently and incorrectly some of the time.

2. *Is this belief logical?*
- Is it sensible to insist that people should do the right thing when they will plainly do the wrong thing again and again?
- If you still believe there is a law which the rest of us don't know about, then it must be your very own law. Does this mean that you are divine? You don't believe that either.
- 'I want people to do the right thing, so they must' doesn't make sense. My definition of correct behaviour will differ

from yours, and everybody else's. Who is right? Nobody, as long as their preferences are stated as demands.

3. *Is it practical to hold this belief? Does thinking this way make it easier or harder for you to achieve your goals?*

- If you demand that people behave competently and correctly (according to your definition), you will probably make yourself feel resentful or hurt when they don't behave to your standards. If you complain about their recalcitrance, you'll get up their noses.
- If you only prefer, even strongly, that people act as you wish, you will never experience anything worse than irritation or disappointment.

New, rational belief

Instead of demanding others to behave well at all times, it would be better to concede that they must get it wrong sometimes, and to think 'What you are doing is inconvenient/unpleasant. I wish you would get it right.' Specific examples of this are:

- 'My teacher is good at what she does, but I wish she weren't so irritable.'
- 'Janine beat me in the exam. Good for her. If she has to swank about it, I think she has a problem.'
- 'I would really like my family to understand what I do, and give me credit for my efforts, but if they won't, they won't.'

10 Life must give me what I want

The irrational belief we are dealing with here is that life must:

(a) be fair to me;
(b) treat me well at all times;
(c) not require me to work hard at anything I don't want to;
(d) give me guarantees that only good things will happen to me, always.

Life would be lovely if it could be like this, but the problem would be opposition from the rest of us, who also want to be running things to suit ourselves, and ordering the universe to deliver unto us only those things we want.

The belief that things should always go well is the basis of worrying. In relation to performance, it creates and perpetuates fear that things will go wrong, and rage and depression when they do, as they sometimes must. The need for guarantees, comfort and success is one of the causes of procrastination. The procrastinator waits for the right moment, or the right feeling, before starting to work.

This belief also leads, for example, to a fear of discomfort (usually anxiety) in musicians who fear the shakes, oral examination candidates who are afraid of becoming inarticulate, people who become nervous before making a speech, and socially anxious people who fear that their anxiety symptoms will prevent them from performing well and so make them look foolish.

As wishing for success and acceptance has some benefits when kept as a preference, so does the wish for things to go right. It leads to a person being alert to the fact that things can go wrong, and encourages the taking of reasonable steps to increase the probability that things will go well. But once the preference becomes elevated to a demand or a must, an infantile reaction ensues. When we whine over things going wrong, we are reverting to childish behaviour, to a time when immature brains and lack of experience did not equip us to understand that we live in a world that is not constructed according to our prescription. That's all right for children; they can get away with it. We adults cannot.

Disputing

The evidence

Is there any evidence to support a belief that things must go as you would like them to? Does the daily paper always bring good news? Do the traffic lights always turn green as you approach them, and when you make a telephone call is the person you want to speak to always there waiting to talk to you? Does equipment never malfunction? Think of those people of whom you most disapprove for their unethical or brutal behaviour. Can your wishing make them succumb to a debilitating disease? If only!

The logic

'I want my life to be smooth, easy, comfortable and with good fortune guaranteed and enduring. So it must be just like that.' Does this make sense? Is it logical? No. It is natural and reasonable to want things to be just like that, but surely you do not believe that you are magical and divine, or even particularly special? Yet you would have to be in order for your wishes to be turned into divine commands.

Be thankful that you don't have the power to make the universe obey your orders. Your commands would affect numerous other people, so you would have to carry huge responsibilities. (On the other hand, if you made things uncomfortable for people, they wouldn't be able to complain, unless you allowed them to.) Please do not take any of this personally. The object of ridicule is not you, but ideas which you may have, and which most of us do subscribe to from time to time. It really does help to treat irrational beliefs as the nonsense that they are.

The practical effects

Ask yourself this — is it likely to help or hinder you to believe that things must go the way you want them to? The answer is obvious by now.

The linking of iBs

The irrational belief that life should be lovely can easily link to other iBs. Let us consider a few examples of this.

1. 'I have practised/rehearsed/studied/trained/worked hard at this, so I should succeed. It would be horrible if I were to fail, and I can't bear to think of it (I can't stand it).' The result of this would be anxiety, because of predicting dire events.

2. 'I am talented, and I work hard, and people should appreciate/value/understand what I do. If they don't, they are a hopeless bunch of idiots.' This would cause resentment (anger) because of the demand on others to behave according to certain rules, and the condemnation of others should they fail to do so.

3. 'When I present for an oral examination/audition/competition I should be comfortable, and never anxious, or at least not very much.' This thought, leading on to awfulising and LFT, would cause anxiety.

4. 'Of course it (life) should be fair. Other people should succeed only if I think they deserve it, and if I don't, then they shouldn't succeed.' This is a demand on life and the universe, and on individuals who are conspicuously non-compliant. And when the individuals disobey, the resulting emotion is usually anger or depression because the demander is thinking 'Life stinks.'

5. 'When I'm as good as other performers, and I work as hard as they do, I should do as well as they do. I'm absolutely fed up (I can't stand it). It's (my life is) horrible.' This thinking would cause self-pitying, depressed feelings.

6. 'I've been trying to lose weight for two months. I've stuck to my diet, and this week I haven't lost a gram. There is no point in trying. Nothing ever works. I'm sick of everything. I give up.' The demand that effort must guarantee success, coupled with the negative view of the speaker's life and future, indicates depressed feelings. The withdrawing behaviour would support that.

7. 'I have to give Jones his farewell present and make a speech for 20 minutes, and I'm knotted up inside. I've got time for a couple of drinks. I need them, as I could not cope otherwise.' This states and implies that comfort is essential.

8. 'I'm stick of studying. Five years to get my degree, when I could be out having fun like everyone else. To make it worse, there is no certainty of a job at the end of it all.' The speaker is complaining that it should be possible to have a good life without having to work and miss out on fun, and there should be a guarantee that the sacrifice will pay off. The probable emotion is resentment (sub-set of anger).

See if you can think of any more examples to add to this list. More importantly, examine your own thinking, looking for instances of where you have made irrational demands on life. When you do come across such beliefs in your own thinking, or when they are expressed by other people, dispute them in your mind, and generate a rational belief to replace the irrational one.

Disputing summary

Things quite often don't work out as we would like them to, and disappointments and setbacks are common. The path to success is often made steeper by uncertainty and difficulties. This can be upsetting to anyone at times. However, if you still find it hard to accept that this is how it must be, and believe it to be different, read on.

1. What is the evidence? Does it support or oppose the belief?

▪ If your life should be easier than it is, anxiety should not happen, and if it does happen it should not be uncomfortable. Then how do we explain that anxiety does happen and is uncomfortable? We cannot. We must assume then, that the evidence does not support the belief.

■ Have you ever seen any evidence anywhere that conflicts with this rule of perfect comfort? If you have, the rule doesn't exist. Meet only one vegetarian mosquito, and there is no longer a rule that mosquitoes must dine on blood.

2. *Is this belief logical?*
■ Life is choc-a-bloc full of events, situations and feelings that we don't want because they are unpleasant and inconvenient.
■ It is not logical to believe that life must be different, just as we want it to be. The truth is, it must be exactly the way it is.
■ Of course you would prefer that life were free of difficulties — wouldn't we all? But does your preference mean that it must be so? It doesn't.

3. *Is it practical to hold this belief? Does thinking this way make it easier or harder for you to achieve your goals?*
■ Will insisting that life must be nice at all times help you cope with difficulties, solve problems and maintain peace of mind? You bet it won't.
■ Accepting that difficulties and problems must arise makes it easier to minimise upset and to attend to them.
■ Whining about how things should be is distressing and distracting for you, and gives the people you gripe to a good reason to avoid your company. When we bear our misfortunes with good grace, people are more likely to offer us support and help.

New, rational belief
Life, the world and all the people in it are imperfect. Things will go wrong, and life will at times treat me unfairly. It is this way because it must be. When things go wrong, I will change what I can, and accept what I cannot.

11 'It's awful' and 'I can't stand it'
(Awfulising and Low Frustration Tolerance)

The two irrational beliefs 'It's awful' and 'I can't stand it', or LFT, form a dynamic duo, as they almost always occur together. It is logical for them to do so; if something is awful, then you obviously can't stand it, and if you can't stand something, then obviously it must be awful, that is, too awful to bear. Further, the irrational belief addressed in the previous chapter, 'Life must give me a good time', could be seen as a close relation to the dynamic duo; now we have a dynamic trio.

'Awfulising' and LFT (Low Frustration Tolerance), the philosophy behind 'I-Can't Stand-It-Itis', are the end-point expression of the demand for a life of nothing but guaranteed ease, pleasure, and assured rewards for effort. Without these demanding beliefs, it would be much harder to see any setback as being awful. You would be much more able to recognise and accept that misfortunes are inevitable, and that we do not choose their type, magnitude and timing.

Awfulising, LFT and Comfort-Demanding Self-Talk

This line of self-talk, that is, being anxious about having uncomfortable physical symptoms of anxiety while giving a lecture, making a speech, performing or facing examiners, for example, is the basis of discomfort anxiety.

A (Activating event) — Giving a lecture, making a speech, performing, facing examiners, and feeling anxious.

B (Self-talk) — 'I've been dreading this. This is horrible. I can't stand it. I'd give anything to be out of here.'

C (Consequences) — Anxiety becomes worse.

This is a closed system, one that reinforces itself. In other words, it is a vicious circle. The thoughts make the symptoms worse, and the symptoms make the thoughts worse, and for this reason, as long as a person stays in the situation, and nothing happens to make things better, the anxiety persists. For some people, performance anxiety is at its worst before they actually start performing, and once they begin, it drops considerably, or even disappears. Their experiences teach them to expect this to happen, so it happens that way.

This thinking can also apply to situations such as 'I absolutely must do well at my exams. If I failed it would be horrible. I can't even bear to think about it.' In this case, it is the situation, and not one's emotional reaction, which is perceived as being horrible.

Although these two irrational beliefs go together, let us consider them separately.

Awfulising

An awful sensation or situation could otherwise be labelled horrible, dreadful, terrible, disastrous, catastrophic, too much, too bad, the end, the pits, at least 100 per cent bad, more than 100 per cent bad. There are no degrees or shades of awful. By general agreement, being tortured slowly to death, or dying slowly of an excruciatingly painful disease, or having this happen to someone you care about, could be described as being awful.

Disputing — Awfulising

The evidence

Leaving aside the colloquial use of the 'awfulising' words such as 'disastrous' 'horrible' 'terrible' ('disastrous party', 'horrible meal', 'terrible work' and so on), there probably have been many times when you have said that something was disastrous, awful, horrible or terrible. But have you ever experienced anything as genuinely bad as the real disasters mentioned above? The reality has always been that the events that have been described so colourfully have been considerably less than awful. This suggests that if you label performance failure as 'awful', you would be wildly exaggerating.

The logic

If you think or say that a feeling or an occurrence is awful or horrible, you will react as if it is, with fear and horror. If you truthfully tell yourself that the same event would be bad or unpleasant or inconvenient, your reaction will be much milder. Because of this, you will have a much better chance of being able to think of what you can do to improve the situation.

We are not suggesting that bad things don't happen, because they obviously do, and if something is bad, it is bad. It can be put somewhere on a scale of badness, with trivial inconveniences at the bottom and real disasters at the top. Here is one possible example of such a scale.

Catastrophe Scale or Horror Barometer
85%–100% Horrible — Real disasters, for example, nuclear holocaust, yourself or a loved one dying slowly of a painful disease.
75% Horrible — Broken marriage.
65% Horrible — Failed relationship. House burned down with loss of all photographs and mementoes.
50% Horrible — Retrenched at work.
10% Horrible — Losing a highly valued personal item.
5% Horrible — Forgetting to attend a social function.

Catastrophe scale exercise

Construct your own catastrophe scale. On the vertical scale, make a mark at 10%, 20%, 30% and so on. Think of some undesirable event, something which has happened, or which could possibly happen to you, to put at each of these marks. As always, do this on paper, and not in your head. There is no such thing as a right or wrong scale, and no one can tell you

---

that you are wrong, but you may later on decide to revise your scale. Now think of an undesirable occurrence, preferably dealing with a performance anxiety situation. It might be yourself feeling severe anxiety symptoms during a music audition or an oral examination, losing an important tennis match and perhaps letting down the team, failing annual examinations and having to repeat a year of university study or giving a lecture to an obviously bored audience. Whatever it is, choose an item that you would normally think of as being awful or terrible.

Now assign this item to some point on the scale where you rationally believe it belongs. Most people, when they carry out this exercise, find that they can put the item much lower than the real disaster class.

In my experience, they commonly take off 20 to 40 points. I (RWF) have seen people take an item from the disaster category and reassign it to the 20% class.

You might think this is just another way of saying that there are plenty of worse things that could happen, and if you do, you are perfectly right. There is nothing wrong with that.

If you are a habitual worrier, you can make regular use of the Catastrophe Scale. Copy yours out on a pocket-sized card. Have it laminated. Carry it with you at all times. Whenever you are worrying, identify what it is that you are telling yourself, look for the awfulising, then ascertain where the feared event would go on your catastrophe scale. Having reduced the perceived badness of the event, you will then be in a better position to start problem-solving and reassuring yourself that you can cope with whatever happens. You may hesitate to do this exercise because if someone were to find your card, they might think you were a little strange. If the thought of that makes you anxious, work out why it would, and consult your Catastrophe Scale in order to see just how bad it would really be. In the unlikely event of the card-discoverer teasing you, it might be unpleasant, but surely it would not be terrible.

The practical effects

If you catastrophise about feeling anxious, performing imperfectly or even badly, it will hinder you because your pre-occupation with the horror of the situation will increase your anxiety and inhibit your ability to think clearly and to act in your best interests. If you tell yourself that your discomfort or a situation is bad, but not too bad, your anxiety will be less and you will be more able to think about how to cope. The best course is to rationally assess how bad a situation will be, and acknowledge that it will be that bad, because there is no point in pretending otherwise. Then get on with things.

LFT (Low Frustration Tolerance or Can't-Stand-It-Itis)

When people say 'I can't stand it', it is intimately linked with a statement about how it would be awful. Sometimes it seems almost artificial to separate the two statements, but as we have just had a look at 'awfulising' in its own, we can now discuss LFT.

LFT can be expressed in different ways, such as:

- 'I can't stand it when my hands sweat when I'm giving a concert';
- 'I can't bear to think of the consequences of failing';
- 'I don't know how I'll cope if I don't get that job';
- 'Why should I have to (I shouldn't have to) put up with all this practice for a lousy competition?';
- 'I would do anything to get out of ...';
- 'If my guests do not enjoy themselves at my dinner party tonight, I will just die.'

Disputing — LFT

The evidence

With that description of the meaning of LFT in mind, what has happened in your life that might have led to your death or dissolution? What adverse events have you experienced, what setbacks, misfortunes, or perhaps even personal tragedies? Have you withstood them? Of course you have — you are alive and sane, and probably mostly coping with most of what happens in your life. Think of other people and the problems and setbacks that they have experienced and ask what has happened to them. Usually they stand it in that they recover from the blow, and then get on with their lives. For most of us, the worst thing that ever happens is the death of someone we love. We grieve, and we recover, and life goes on. But some people react much worse than this to much lesser events, for example, being rejected or experiencing a serious setback in business. As you no doubt have already worked out, the reason why they react so badly to a lesser setback is because of their beliefs and their self-talk, not the event itself.

So, just as you have stood everything that has happened to you in your life, you can comfortably predict that you will stand whatever happens in the future, including whatever you might be afraid of right now. Will you stand it? Yes, almost certainly.

The logic

Is it logical, and does it make sense, to believe that if something doesn't go the way you want it to, you can't stand it? Try saying it aloud and thoughtfully. Make up your own phrase, something like one of these examples:

- When my cooking for a formal dinner party is not marvellous, I absolutely cannot stand it, and if it happens too much it will kill me.
- To have to give up time to study (practise, or train) when I could be out enjoying myself with friends is absolutely unbearable. I will certainly go mad.
- It is totally beyond my capacity for endurance if I muck up that third movement of the sonata at tonight's performance. I will disintegrate and crumble into dust.

Of course it looks ridiculous, and it is, but it is just another way of saying 'I can't stand it.' Now, think of any situation that you become anxious about, and which you tell yourself is awful and you can't stand it. Change your language to replace 'I can't stand it' with some phrase like those above. Is there a difference? We expect not. As with all other irrational thinking, LFT is absolutist and rigid, allowing for no shades of meaning or degrees of distress. And therein lies its capacity for damage. Is it the same for everybody? Are there some people who are able to cope, perhaps even comfortably, with things that you can't stand and are there things you cope with which other people become frantic about? If something can't be stood, then surely this would be a quality intrinsic to that something, which would mean that everyone could not stand it. For example, everyone who is decapitated loses his head. The 'not-standing-it' is something within the person, in his or her individual self-talk.

Instead of telling yourself that you can't stand something, tell yourself that no matter how undesirable or unpleasant it is, and how uncomfortable you may become, you can stand it, just as you have stood every other inconvenience and misfortune in your life.

Anti-awfulising and LFT exercise

One exercise is to think of one of your own situations where you procrastinate, or want to give up, or tell yourself that you are fed up, where you are despairing, overwhelmed or helpless. Listen for your self-talk, particularly attending to themes of awfulising and LFT. Change your self-talk to rational anti-awfulising and rational anti-LFT self-talk. Persist with this for a minute or so, and note how your feelings become more comfortable, and how the situation stops looking worse than bad.

It will take you only three or four minutes to do this exercise, and you may need to repeat it 20 or 30 or more times over several days or weeks in order for it to work. The total amount of exposure time is extremely important — the more the better. Apply this exercise to any situation that you are anxious about, and where you procrastinate, avoid, or want to avoid. Procrastination will be dealt with more fully in Chapter 13.

The practical effects

What effect does it have on your performance for you to tell yourself that you can't stand the way you feel about some inconvenience or something unpleasant about the performance?

Would it help you or hinder you, when you want to get down to the work of practising or training, when you need to front up to a test or contest, when you need to concentrate, focus your attention, be task-oriented, tolerate physical discomfort, make the best effort you can, and hang in there and see things through to the finish? The answer is obvious. Telling yourself that you can't stand anything leads to anxiety, and perhaps anger. Anxiety can escalate to panic if you tell yourself that you cannot stand the anxiety feelings that you already have. You are more likely to feel despair, to have a sense of hopelessness and to give up too easily. Can't-Stand-It-Itis is the prime cause of avoidance, so LFT is much more likely to lead to not trying, giving up easily, or leaving the situation altogether.

On the other hand, if you tell yourself that a situation or event is unpleasant, but it is not in any way too bad, and you can stand it, the effect will be one of better control over your feelings, better concentration, more intense focusing on the task, problem-solving where this is needed, and a capacity to endure. And the anticipation is nearly always worse than the event itself.

Disputing summary

If you become anxious, miserable or angry because your life's circumstances are not as you want them to be, and you think that you have too many hassles and difficulties, ask yourself how many problems and discomforts you are supposed to have? Is there a National Standard for Comfort and Convenience that applies to our lives? If you want to make a formal complaint, to which government department do you send it? You can learn to stand whatever happens to you or to those close to you, and it is rarely likely to be awful, meaning too bad. And certainly, a performance challenge can never be too bad.

1. What is the evidence? Does it support or oppose the belief?
You have heard yourself say that you couldn't stand it, bear it, put up with it, and so on. You have heard others say the same things. What does this mean — that you would die, go mad, be vaporised? If not that, then what, or does it mean nothing at all, while sounding drastic? And what did happen on those occasions? You are, we presume still alive, and well. You stood it. Your

predictions were wrong. The evidence of the past suggests that you will probably stand whatever happens to you in your life.

2. Is this belief logical?
If you don't like something — effort, delay, discomfort, unfairness, anything — can this mean that it will be absolutely unbearable, that it will kill or maim you? No. Is everyone on Earth unable to stand the things you can't stand? No. Can some people cope adequately, or even well, with things you claim you can't stand, and vice versa? Has your ability to stand some things changed? Probably. With this in mind, can anyone logically claim that they, uniquely in the whole world, will collapse and die if they do badly at something and feel uncomfortable about it? You know the answer. It is a crazy notion. LFT and awfulising beliefs don't make sense.

3. Is it practical to hold this belief? Does thinking this way make it easier or harder for you to achieve your goals?
If you'd rather not feel afraid of anxiety, impatient with delay, resentful at 'unfairness', terrified of failing, then what had you better believe?

   (a) If anything like that happened it would be awful and I couldn't stand it, or

   (b) I certainly wouldn't like it, but these things happen, and I can stand it. I'll cope.

No prizes for choosing (b). If you like a bit of suffering now and then, go for (a). You will be on a winner.

New, rational belief

In life, things will happen that will be inconvenient, annoying, uncomfortable, painful or just plain bad. There will be delays, frustrations, unfairness and the need to make an effort in order to gain what I want. That's life, it is the way it must be, and it's okay the way it is. It is irrational and a waste of time to whine about things I don't like, because they are rarely terrible, and I can stand whatever happens just as I have always stood misfortunes in the past.

12 Global Rating

**Man who does not suffer fools gladly
deserve yak dung pie in face.**
(Tibetan proverb)

It is impossible to put a value on a human being. Anyone who rates his worth on the basis of how well he does something, or for any reason at all, is giving himself and others an unnecessarily hard time.

The usual reason why people demand that they must perform excellently (or whatever standard they set for themselves) is that they relate their worth as a person to how well or badly they do something. Humans do very well at thinking negatively and irrationally, so it is hardly ever a case of positive irrational thinking as in 'I must come top in that exam and so prove that I'm a thoroughly fine chap.' More often, the thinking is negatively irrational — 'I must come top in that exam because if I don't, I will have failed, and that would mean I am a failure.'

The cause of anxiety is the danger of being proved to be a failure, stupid, hopeless, worthless and so on. The victim is to be consigned to complete, utter and total rottendom, and no half measures, nothing partial, will be allowed. According to whether we approve or disapprove of a person's actions, we confer nobility or ignobility on him. Once there, he stays there until we decide to revise his status. To add to his problems, it is far easier to descend the scale of virtue than to be rehabilitated. And we do it to ourselves as enthusiastically as we do it to others.

As many of us are strongly inclined to globally rating ourselves, other people and the things we and they do, pursuing the harmful and illogical rating game, it is worth considering why we do this. One reason is that we like things to be easy, and globally rating a person or an act is easier than thinking analytically and expressing ourselves thoughtfully about that person or act. How much easier and more satisfying to call someone lazy than to think about why he is behaving the way he is, and to consider this in the light of his overall circumstances. Labelling someone negatively helps us to feel superior, or at least adequate. Giving someone a total positive rating is also good for us, if we see them as having something in common with ourselves.

What about you in this matter? If you globally rate yourself, as most of us do, how can you set about disputing this line of thinking? In a previous chapter we used as an example someone who wants to do well in an examination, get a promotion at work, or impress an audience, and is anxious about it. We said the self-talk would probably be 'I must do well because to not do so is to fail, which would make me a failure.' This demand on oneself to succeed is linked to global self-rating, that is the fear of being shown to be a failure.

The problem with global rating is that it is global, total, complete and utter, black and white. If you are worthless, incompetent, or a failure, you think you are that, totally, and by definition, unable to do anything sensibly, competently or successfully, or to have any worth. This is not only extreme, it's absolute. If you call yourself stupid, for example, you are thinking of yourself as being just that, stupid, without any sensibility.

If you believe that you are in danger of being relegated to failure because of doing badly at anything, remember, as a total failure you aren't allowed to do anything at all successfully.

Disputing

The evidence

All the evidence in the world can never prove that someone is a total success or a total failure. However, if someone is globally rated as a failure, he or she must be a total failure in everything he or she has ever attempted.

Look at some facts. Have you ever succeeded at anything? Of course you have, so think of one or two instances now, but don't (a) say they don't count, or (b) start calling yourself a success. This is not an exercise in what to call yourself, but in developing your awareness of the concept that facts matter.

If you were a lawyer in court, defending your client who had been charged with being a total failure, and the prosecution's case consists only of 'She did poorly in an examination, Your Honour', would you give up at that point, because you had no case, no evidence that the client had ever succeeded at anything?

At a more mundane level, would you listen to a friend calling herself a loser and a failure because she thought she might perform badly at something, and not remind her of what she does competently and well? Be a friend to yourself, be your own defence lawyer. Be scientific, and ask yourself what the evidence is, evaluate each item and seek a balanced view. Rate what you do — your deeds — but never yourself.

The logic

This certainly is at the heart of disputing the global rating of persons. It is not possible to prove, by using logic, that a human being has some, much, a lot of worth, or none at all. It follows that what a person does, and how well or badly they do it, can never be an indicator of what they are as a whole person, because that is something that cannot be defined, measured or changed.

It is not logical to take a person, and assign to him or her a ranking on a scale of human worth or value, for any reason at all. At this point you may or may not be able to accept this. If you can, good, but if you can't yet, we hope you will be convinced eventually, as we cannot overrate the importance of our succeeding in this task. Believing that it is possible to evaluate the worth of oneself or others is a major source of anxiety, depression and anger.

This chapter deals with the pressures we put on ourselves to perform a task excellently, in order to avoid being proved a failure, or worthless in some way. This suggests that the task, say, giving an interesting talk on weed control, is the yardstick of 'worthwhileness'. But what about all our other qualities and abilities, such as our appearance, personality and intelligence? Each of us has so many attributes and aspects that no one item can possibly measure of your worth.

Dot exercise

Take a blank sheet of paper, and with a pencil start marking dots anywhere on it. Each dot represents one aspect of yourself, good, bad or neutral, whether you like or dislike it, or have no preference. Start with your appearance if you wish, and you might as well begin at the top and work your way down. Do you have some hair? Dot. Is it fine or coarse? Dot. What is the colour? Dot. Is it straight or curly? Dot. Do people compliment you on it? Dot. Now for your forehead. Is it high or low? Dot. Is it noble or Neanderthal? Dot. Is it wrinkled or smooth? Dot. That's quite a few dots, and you haven't reached your eyebrows and ears. The page will be starting to look rather spotty by the time you get to the soles of your feet. After that, you can move on to all the many other aspects of yourself. If you follow this exercise right through to its end, the page will be extremely spotty. How do you find the end, anyway? Perhaps you stop when you run out of space for dots or you need a new pencil.

Of course you don't need to persist with this exercise until you run out of time, paper or patience. Its purpose is to help you understand more fully that you have an almost infinite number of characteristics, of greater and lesser importance, which you will evaluate in different ways.

Is there any one characteristic that defines you? Is there any single dot on the page which you could point to and say 'That represents my worth as a person'?

Let us say your talk on weed control is well received, and you are pleased with it. You liked the way you sounded, and the audience responded well. You have proved your worth. Then you find that several people were confused by your talk, and your presentation irritated them. Horror! You are now less worthwhile. Then you discover that they thought you were someone else, and that the lecture was about flower arranging. Relief! They were wrong, and you are still worthwhile.

Next month, you give the same talk to a different audience, who are obviously unimpressed. Now you are a failure. But what if they were ignorant of the topic, and not qualified to judge your talk? You didn't fail, and are saved from the Pit of Worthlessness.

Over two years, you give 15 talks. The quality varies. Do you become a better and worse person as the standard goes up and down? Practice improves your performance; do you become a better person? When you retire from lecturing, will you then have no worth at all, or can you rest on your worthwhile laurels?

As it happens, your best friends have little interest in horticulture, and never give lectures at all. Does this make them worthless, if giving interesting lectures is the yardstick of human excellence? Surely you would not judge your friends this way, so why do it to yourself?

Your friends hear your tormented self-condemnation after one of your dud lectures. They try to comfort you by telling you that you are much more than a flower-lover and occasional lecturer, and they describe the qualities they like you for, and the things you do well. If you dismiss what they say, and insist that you are right and they are wrong, is this not grandiose? How do you know that you are right? If you are such a worm, surely you can't be right, in which case you had better stop torturing yourself, and believe what they tell you.

But wait. A dispute has broken out among your committee of cheerer-uppers:

C-U 1 'She's a great cook, and as a food-lover, I think that is what counts. I value her.'
C-U 2 'Rubbish! Your stomach is not the judge of her worth. She has been very kind to me, a true friend, and that is what matters. Love, and beans on toast for me!'

C-U 3 'How self-centred! Your stomach, and your love needs! What I value her for is her kindness. She works for charity, and helps little old ladies cross the street. But as a businesswoman, I did lose respect for her when her flower shop failed.'

C-U 4 'That's ridiculous. Those things don't matter. Anyone can learn to cook, and be kind and nice if they want to, in order to win approval. You three are a bunch of soft-headed nitwits if you believe that pap. Perhaps she is a rotten lecturer — I don't care about that. What I admire and respect her for is that she keeps on trying at whatever she does. She's got grit. Where would the world be if it weren't for people with faith in themselves and a drive to get ahead?'

And so on to:
C-U 127 'That's 126 different opinions, and they're all different. Perhaps we can't ever reach agreement because there is no universally accepted yardstick for measuring a person's worth, and it cannot be measured. Any attempt to do so is a waste of time. I suggest we encourage her to accept herself as intrinsically worthwhile simply because she exists, and tell her that whatever her worth is, it cannot be defined, measured, changed or taken away from her. She can be pleased about what she does well, and regret what she does badly, including giving thoroughly rotten lectures. But that is as far as it goes. It has nothing to do with what she is.'

All, in chorus: 'You are absolutely right! How wise! How sensible! How rational!'

Apart from discovering that there are 127 people who care about you, you would have also learned that:

- no one yet has been able to define the worth of a human being;
- no one yet has been able to state what it is;
- no one yet has been able explain how to measure it;
- no one yet has been able to tell how it can be increased or reduced;
- anyone who has tried, as above, has not managed to convince anyone else that they have succeeded.

So it is plain that the only logical (and practical) thing to do is to stop trying.

This leaves you able to enjoy succeeding, and to be disappointed by failure, but never thinking that what you do reflects or changes your worth as a person. Who and what you are is stable, unassailable and secure. Nothing can take away your worth. This includes what you think, say or do, what happens to you, what others say about you, what they think of you, or do to you.

That's all right for us ordinary folks, but what about A. Hitler, J. Stalin, assorted murderers and narcotics tycoons? How can they not be classed as not inferior to decent people? Surely there are standards? Many people, very reasonably, get stuck on this point. But ask yourself, how does it help you or society for you to judge any of these people as inferior? If there is a line, below which a person's actions are unacceptable, so that if he commits deeds in that grisly or sadistic zone he puts himself down to a level where he can be judged as an inferior person, then who sets that standard? There cannot be universal agreement as to what the standard is. It will vary from time to time in human history, from one society to another and between individuals.

This brings us to another important aspect of the global rating business — the belief that what (we imagine) others think of us determines whether we are wise or stupid, bright or dumb, beautiful or hideous, charismatic or boring, a good or hopeless performer, and so on. This belief is the basis of our need for approval and acceptance, as in 'I have to impress Suzy when we go out for dinner, because if she thinks I'm a drag, then I must be one.' This is often part of performance anxiety — the belief that one needs to succeed in order to gain approval, which in turn will prove that the performer is worthwhile. The belief that what anyone thinks of us can somehow constitute what we are is illogical, and hence irrational.

Once you globally rate yourself because of what someone might think of you, then a few questions must be asked. What if someone else thinks differently? What happens if the person changes their mind? How are they qualified to have this golden insight into your essence? Do you believe that what you think of others is necessarily a true reflection of who they are and how capable and talented they are? Sometimes I (RWF) am told 'I am a performer, and I need an audience. If people are so unimpressed that they stay away, then I have no audience, in which case I have no career. Surely I exist as a musician only by virtue of what people think of me?' Does this mean that the speaker does not exist as a human being because the world is full of people who do not know he is alive? In a practical sense, if a musician as a performer never has an audience, then surely it is time for him to do something different, such as improving his skills, or changing his job. However, the absent audiences' collective opinions reflect, and do not create, his talents or his worth.

The practical effects

Believing that how well you do, or what someone thinks of you, has the power to make you completely clever/talented/able/brilliant/virtuously tenacious, or their complete opposites, may have some beneficial effects. It may help raise your level of arousal by making you anxious. This arousal may help you concentrate effectively and may make you work harder and persist longer.

That's good, but the cost is anxiety, even terror, brought on by the belief that to fail or be disapproved of is proof of one's inferiority. Instead of having only one goal, such as an examination or contest to focus on, there is the second one — the need to prove that one does not belong to some lower order of life. This is much more cosmic, and can be more than a little distracting.

Succeeding in the face of such danger may lead to great relief, perhaps exultation. But this cannot last; knowing that you must always succeed at this level, because one failure will condemn you to total failurehood, is enough to destroy anyone's peace of mind.

Whatever benefits come from these drastic beliefs are bought at a very high price indeed. And it need not be so.

For those who insist that anxiety is essential for their best performance, that they must succeed and/or be applauded, and that a substandard performance = failure and personal inadequacy, here are some interesting facts:

- Some people succeed admirably without ever being afraid of failing.
- The most terrified performers do not perform at their best.
- People are more likely to give up competing and performing because of performance anxiety than because of calmly

underachieving. If they are frank, they say that it wasn't worth the (self-inflicted) agony.

■ Losing performance anxiety nearly always leads to better performance.

■ Those who lose their performance anxiety never regret doing so. They almost always insist that life has become much more agreeable.

Finally, look at the other side of the coin. Is it essential to evaluate the worth of other people in order for you to be able to lead a happy life? How does it increase your happiness for you to consider yourself or anyone else as worthless, mediocre or totally worthwhile, for any reason whatsoever? How would refusing to be in the rating game make your life unsatisfying and unhappy? How do you rate someone's worth? Can it be done effectively? You could drive yourself bonkers trying to think of a universally acceptable way of doing it. Meanwhile, move out of the rating game altogether for a while, and see how it feels by doing the no-rating exercise.

The no-rating exercise

This exercise can be revealing to those of us who frequently criticise others (and ourselves), but are not aware of it, because it seems as natural as breathing.

Here is how it is done. Try to be as non-judgemental as you can be, about people, situations, and so on, for a day, then a week or so. After that time, reflect on your experience with this exercise, and decide if you have felt any benefits. Think of it this way: if you are usually critical of many people and things, then you must also be critical of yourself much of the time. The no-rating exercise may help you be more tolerant of yourself, with all the usual human imperfections you possess. In addition, you may begin to feel more kindly and understanding towards your family, friends and others as a result of your non-judgemental attitudes. You may decide that adopting more tolerant attitudes to the annoying people and situations that turn up in your life so much of the time enhances your life as much as anybody else's.

Here are a few annoying situations in which you could practise the no-rating exercise.

- When you find yourself caught in a conversation with people whose political/social views are diametrically opposite to yours, don't judge them as a conscienceless fools. They are, just like you, the product of many influences. Express your disagreement with the views and change the subject. Let them be.

- Think of your most unfavourite public figure. Think about what he/she is doing that concerns you, and try not to judge this person. Take the view that, given their life circumstances and influences (about which you probably know little), they must do what they are doing. They probably believe that they are acting in the only possible way, even when you consider their behaviour to be unethical.

- When you next hear objectionable music (to you) roaring from a car near you, stop yourself from condemning the driver as a self-absorbed halfwit. You may despise his taste in music and antisocial behaviour, but he surely believes that what he is doing is reasonable, even the best that he can do at that time.

- Think of a former friend who has hurt you very badly. You may not understand why she behaved hurtfully towards you; but there are probably many things about that person which you won't ever know or understand. Try not to judge. She behaved as well as she could (given her needs, about which you probably knew little) at the time, and so did you.

- When people you know are judging and condemning a mutual acquaintance, defend the person, and see if you can change the critical tone of the conversation.

- Think of someone you know who rarely criticises anyone. Does this person come across as a milk-sop, without any opinions of his own? Almost certainly not. Think about this one.

Disputing summary

It is easy, and tempting, to globally (totally) rate the worth of human beings, including ourselves. It is tempting because it is easy, and it is easy because it is a simple way of thinking, and we are all inclined to laziness and irrational thinking. Such thinking leads to the ready condemnation of others and ourselves, and hence to anger, anxiety and depression. Performance anxiety is almost always associated with the tendency to rate oneself according to the quality of one's performance, so look for the tendency in yourself. The truth is that we are all fallible. Give up on the idea of rating yourself or anyone else, and focus not on the quality of a person, but on the quality of their (and your) deeds.

1. *What is the evidence?*
* If you decide that any person is inferior, stupid, worthless, hopeless, talentless, or whatever else, then look at the facts about that person. If someone is stupid, then he can only ever act stupidly, and not sensibly. Do the facts of his life support this?
* Remember, if you are a failure, you are a total failure and not a partial failure. These words do mean something. If you have ever exhibited abilities or talents, then there is enough evidence to disprove any statement that you are totally without ability or talent. If you are a failure, then you must never have succeeded at anything you have attempted. Is this true?

2. *Is this thinking logical?*
* If a person performs badly in one area, does it make sense to say that he is completely bad in that area, or in any other aspect of his life?
* If you happen to bore someone for a few minutes, does this mean that you are a bore, meaning totally boring and no one could ever find you interesting?
* If you succeed at something today, does it make you a success, and then when you don't do so well at the same thing tomorrow you have become a failure overnight? Is that possible?
* If two people have radically different opinions of you or your abilities, are you in danger of splitting down the middle into two completely incompatible halves — hopeless and excellent?

- If someone's opinion of you changes, do you change as a result?
- If your worth as a person can logically be changed or measured by how well you do something or what people think of you, does this happen only to you? Or is the whole human race in the same situation?
- If someone loves and adores you, does that make you totally lovable, and adorable? And when that person falls out of love with you, do you become unlovable?
- Do you judge other people, totally, because of one or several of their academic, artistic or sporting performances?

3. Is this thinking practical?
In order for you to perform well at anything, it is in your interests to be aroused and alert, but definitely unafraid. Fear and terror only inhibit good performance. If your worth as a person, your entitlement to be considered fit to belong to the human race, depends on your performing well at anything, then there is an enormous amount at stake every time you try and might fail. You will be striving not just to succeed or win, or do well, but to stay out of hell. Believing this will certainly get in the way of best performance, and even if you do well, your success will come at the cost of extremely high anxiety. If you fail, get ready to beat yourself up and become depressed. Even if you succeed, there will always be the next time.

Now memorise and incorporate into your belief system the New Rational Belief. To reinforce it, start doing the No-Rating Exercise.

New, rational belief

Try believing that you prefer to succeed enough of the time, and that you hope your efforts will be approved of by enough people who matter to you, but that this doesn't have any bearing on your intrinsic worth, because this cannot be described, defined, measured or changed in any way. This is true for everybody. Believe that, and you will find it much easier to have a happy life, without any guarantees (but you can stand that).

13 Procrastination

Procrastination is avoidance

Procrastination means putting things off instead of doing them promptly. Everyone procrastinates, and has low frustration tolerance, at least a little. Procrastinating results when we wrongly tell ourselves that a task is too unpleasant to do, or even to think about.

There is 'normal' procrastination, but problem procrastination causes overdue and ill-prepared work. This irritates others, and causes the procrastinator anxiety, inconvenience and last-minute frantic cramming or practising. His late work is penalised, and his negative beliefs about his abilities and himself are reinforced.

Procrastinating is avoidance, a potent reinforcer of anxiety. When Percy the procrastinator thinks of working on his assignment, he becomes anxious or glum. He puts work out of his mind, and thinks of doing something more pleasant (or less aversive). He then feels more comfortable; losing his discomfort reinforces the probability that he will do the same again. This short-term pleasure is more powerful than the delayed pain of procrastinating. Humans often get that equation wrong; they don't pay the electricity bill, so the power is cut off, and they perform badly because they put off studying and practising. Not smart, is it? Percy's procrastinating method is a popular one. Think of all the students who spend their evenings watching television or playing computer games instead of studying.

There are other procrastinating styles. Are any of these yours?

- Making unnecessary preparations, for example reading a book on decorating, and visiting five paint shops, before painting the back fence.
- Doing other necessary and virtuous (but less urgent and certainly less unpleasant) tasks first — they get a priority upgrade.
- Preparing yourself for tackling a task you dislike by, for example, saying, 'I'll have a good long session of relaxation before I make that phone call — I'll handle it better then.'
- Doing other things, just for a few minutes, then becoming absorbed in them, and forgetting about the main task.
- Waiting until the time is right or you are ready and you 'feel right'. When do you ever feel good about doing something you don't want to do? The good feeling comes after you have done it.
- Seriously believing yourself when you think/say, 'I can't get started until just before an assignment is due — I need the adrenalin rush.' Do you also need the intestinal rush, palpitations, tremors, fear and insomnia?
- Putting off everything until the right time or the right circumstances, instead of doing things when the need arises.
- Daydreaming of glory; this can be quite absorbing, and a satisfying alternative to action.

The self-talk that underlies procrastination

There are different patterns of self-talk for procrastinators, because people have different reasons for wanting to procrastinate. Rationalising (giving oneself an apparently good, but actually false, reason) is common.

1. - Activating event — the task is boring, tedious or frustrating.
   - Consequences — anxiety and anger.
   - Beliefs and self-talk — 'It's awful.' (Awfulising)
     'And I hate it.' (Can't-Stand-It-Itis, or LFT)
     'I shouldn't have to do it.' (The world should always be kind to me)

> *Anti-procrastinating rational statement:* 'This task is tedious, but not awful. I don't like it, but I can stand doing it. There is no law that says I shouldn't have to do it, so let's get on with it. I will enjoy completing the task.'

2. ■ Activating event — thinking that others have set excessively high standards or imposed disagreeable tasks or 'unfair' conditions, or don't appreciate your effort.
   ■ Consequences — resentment, anger, delaying, complying without commitment or enthusiasm.
   ■ Beliefs and self-talk —
   'It's unfair.' (Life should be fair)
   'They should treat me better.' (Others should treat me as I want them to)
   'They are a bunch (herd) of swine.' (Global rating)
   'I should punish them (for breaking my rules).'

> *Anti-procrastinating rational statement:* 'I don't like these conditions, but that doesn't mean it shouldn't be like this, or that they must treat me better. I don't make the rules, so I might as well accept them. I don't like their behaviour, but that doesn't mean that they are no good, or that I should punish them by delaying.'

3. ■ Activating event — You are about to try, but your efforts may disappoint you or be criticised.
   ■ Consequences — anxiety, avoidance.
   ■ Beliefs and self-talk —
   'I must succeed.' (Demand on oneself to succeed)
   'But I might fail.' (Fact)
   'Then I would be a failure.' (Global rating)
   or
   'My efforts should be approved of.' (Need for approval)
   'But they may not be.' (Fact)
   'Their disapproving of my efforts would prove that I am a failure.' (Global rating)

> *Anti-procrastinating rational statement:* 'I hope to succeed and/or have people approve of what I do because there are obvious benefits, but there is no law to say that either of these must happen. Whatever happens, it has no bearing on my worth as a person, which can't ever be measured or changed.'

Other causes of procrastination

- Taking on inappropriate commitments because of being unable to say 'no'. This leads to a person's being overloaded and anxious and perhaps resentful about having to do anything. She might at first feel angry with herself for her non-assertiveness, and then transfer that anger to the people who have asked her to do things, telling herself that they 'should have been able to see' that she was already too busy. The resulting procrastination may be a passive-aggressive response to her resentful fear of displeasing the people who have made requests of her, or of being a failure if she cannot cope with the requests, or simple fatigue.
- Some people take on tasks that they then procrastinate over, and very slowly come to realise that they don't really want to do the work. I (RWF) recently treated a young man who could not motivate himself to work on his postgraduate thesis. After several months of no response to treatment, he announced that he had decided to abandon the thesis, because he realised that he was not interested enough in the topic and saw no benefit in acquiring a postgraduate degree.
- When we procrastinate over working on a commitment, it does not go away. The task that needs to be done continues to need to be done. Avoidance generates more avoidance. The situation grows worse because more items can be added to the task, or the time to completion shrinks, so the work becomes harder, which creates more anxiety and even more pressure to procrastinate.

What to do about procrastination

First, ask where is the problem — in this task, or in you? If it is the latter, have you always procrastinated, or have you changed, and become 'lazy'? If this is a new problem for you, could you be depressed? If you are, it must be tackled. See Chapter 16.

If you have a major problem with procrastination, you will probably need to take a thorough approach to overcoming it. You could start by reading one of the several good books on the subject, such as *Do It Now* by Dr. William Knaus (see the Bibliography at the back of the book). However, if you procrastinate to just a 'normal' extent, the following suggestions may help.

Begin by recognising that your procrastination is a problem for you, whether it is open and obvious, or covert and seemingly virtuous. Covert procrastination happens when the procrastinator gets involved in excessive preparations, or in activities that appear necessary but aren't, or in giving others help they don't need. He feels good while he is thus engaged, because he mostly believes himself when he proclaims that he must do what he is doing. This stratagem works for a while, because the procrastinator is conning himself, but, to paraphrase Abraham Lincoln, 'You can't fool yourself all the time.'

Both cognitive and behavioural techniques need to be employed in nearly every case. Procrastination is manifestly a behavioural disturbance. Using the methods which you are now familiar with, find the self-talk that causes the anxiety that causes and guides the avoiding behaviour, dispute it, and generate new, rational beliefs. Continue doing this whenever you need to. Use whatever methods you find helpful to drill yourself in learning to think rationally. This should help you change your behaviour, but it does not guarantee that you will.

Here are some things you can try. Because there are different procrastinating styles, you may need to try different techniques in order to find what helps you.

■ *Play the role of the non-procrastinator*
For one week undertake to do absolutely everything as soon as the need arises, no matter what it is — ironing your shirt, paying a bill, making a difficult telephone call, studying, practising the piano, going to bed at the right time — everything. No excuses, no exceptions. Before you start, convince yourself, if you need to, that you have nothing to lose by doing this. It may help you to act out a role, to be in

the character of someone who always does everything straight away. By the end of the week you may have replaced your bad habit with a good one, to some extent, but you won't be cured. You could be feeling happier and calmer, which will probably reinforce your smarter behaviour. Commit yourself to a second week of the same. And keep on doing it. The aim of this is not to make you into a compulsive non-procrastinator, but to break the habit for long enough for you to experience the pleasure brought by non-procrastinating behaviour, so you can choose to adopt, or reject, a new set of attitudes.

■ *Do a cost/benefit analysis*
Analysing the costs and benefits of procrastinating (and other actions) is often helpful. It simply involves listing the advantages and disadvantages of a course of action and its alternative(s). The basic form is two columns; record the pros and cons, and then see which side is the more convincing. It is essential to write, and not to try making it a mental exercise, for good reasons given earlier.

You may need to take it further, by doing a hedonic calculus, in which you examine your thoughts more thoroughly. See the example on page 118, Fig 13.1.

The hedonic calculus is useful in a wide range of situations, such as deciding whether to undertake a long course of study, or take a new job, where there are doubts about what to do.

In each column, you can write the points randomly, or try to line them up with related ideas in other columns. It doesn't really matter. If you start with Column A, don't just stop when you finish Column D; when you run out of ideas, read each column, and what you see there might give you more ideas. You may do better if someone else helps; perhaps you can brainstorm — their thoughts stimulate yours, and vice versa. Despite the name, there is no calculating, because it isn't necessary; it is usually obvious that the rational thoughts are valid, and the irrational ones are false or feeble, so the rational ideas clearly win.

A Advantages of Procrastinating	B Disadvantages of procrastinating	C. Advantages of studying consistently and not procrastinating	D Disadvantages of studying consistently and not procrastinating
1. More time to do things I like to do.	1. I always feel uncomfortable knowing that I'm messing around instead of studying.	1. I feel good when I'm up to date with my work.	1. I have to delay my recreations and pleasures — big deal!
2. I hate studying, so I feel more comfortable when I don't study.	2. I do prefer watching TV, etc to studying, but I'd enjoy them more if I studied first.	2. When I'm up to date I can fully enjoy the fun things.	
3. I can enjoy myself now, and catch up later.	3. I might leave my run too late, and do badly.	3. By working calmer and working better, I can get better marks.	
4. I won't be a swot. Swots are uncool.	4. Trying to catch up is hard work.	4. It pleases my family.	
5. I can spend more time on my computer. I think I'd rather be working on my computer — maybe that's where my future lies anyway.	5. I'll be uncomfortable while I'm delaying, and very uncomfortable when I have to cram before examinations.	5. It helps me to develop self-discipline and see myself as a person who copes.	
	6. It's just stupid.		
	7. Being late, doing badly and failing are extremely uncool.		
	8. My parents will nag me and that's unpleasant.		

Fig 13.1 *Hedonic Calculus*

If you can see no clear advantage to one side or the other, that is, A+D versus B+C, go through it carefully, questioning and challenging each point; some statements may become stronger, and some weaker.

There is one possibility to consider. If you do a hedonic calculus for whether it is best to get on with studying a certain subject, climbing the ladder at work, or whatever, and you cannot come up with a clear conclusion, one possibility is that you are not, in your heart, interested in doing whatever it is. If this might be the case, then do a hedonic calculus for that topic, the long-term goal. For example, note the advantages and disadvantages of, say, working for over 60 hours a week in order to become a manager within the next five years.

Prepare a pocket-sized card. On one side summarise the points from the hedonic calculus for, and on the other side, the points against, doing something; for example, procrastinating. Carry the card, and read it thoughtfully 10 or more times a day.

Some techniques to facilitate behaviour change

1) Make a commitment. Tell one or two other people whom you respect that you intend to complete an assignment by a certain date.

Make the commitment stronger by nominating a penalty to pay if you do not meet your goal. For instance, you could undertake to mow their lawns or wash their car; the penalty must matter to you, but not too much. It needs to cause you significant, but not excessive, discomfort. You could lodge a $50 or $100 bill with your friend and tell her to burn it (and show you the ashes) on the due date if you don't meet the deadline. If you can't bear the thought of burning money, an alternative is for you to post it to a cause you despise. For added spice, include a note, written in advance, complimenting the group or cause on their good work.

On the positive side, you can arrange to reward yourself with pleasant events or sums of money for completion of each module of your work. If it is money, decide what the grand reward is to be, and when you have earned it, collect it promptly, as delaying weakens the reinforcing effect of a reward.

2) If you have a habit of wasting a lot of time by doing little bits of this and that, things that you can't even recall at the end of the day, start a diary, preferably an appointment book, where the day is divided up into blocks of time, say one hour. At the end of each interval, record briefly what you have done. At the end of each day, and each week, review what you have been doing. Combine this book with a plan, in which you allocate specific times and amounts of time for the necessary maintenance tasks such as eating, sleeping, washing your socks and leisure and pleasure activities. You are much more likely to enjoy, and benefit from, leisure activities if they are taken at planned times and have been 'earned' by doing necessary tasks.

3) If a job is very big, you might procrastinate because of its overall magnitude. Remember the old Chinese proverb, 'A journey of 1000 miles starts with a single step', which although obvious, is helpful to remember. So break the task down into smaller components, and deal with them in order. If you are going for a picnic in the country, or on a holiday, you have to plan it. You don't just pile into the car and head off down the street without any food, drink, utensils, money, or any idea of where you are going. It is not the same as planning as trip to the moon, but you plan, just the same. Start with the big picture, 'Let's have a picnic on Sunday', and then work on the small details. A task more complex than scratching your head can be broken down into its components; this applies to any project you undertake. Perhaps the whole project looks very big and daunting, and as long as you keep on thinking of it only as a whole project, it will continue to daunt you. But you can divide and sub-divide and sub-sub-divide it, until you reduce it to manageable portions.

4) If you have a goal which is a week, a month, six months or a year or more away, work out what are the components, and the intermediate goals. For each intermediate goal, work out what you can do each month, each week, and each day. Record these as tasks in your diary. Each day's tasks will be quite small, in fact minute, compared with the overall task. If your project is to lose 20 kilograms in one year, and to become physically fit in that

time, these are major goals. If the changes took place overnight, you would not recognise yourself, how you looked or felt, the next morning. If your diary commits you to recording your daily calorie intake, keeping it at 1500–2000, walking briskly for 20 minutes each day, ensuring that you get enough sleep each night, and spending 45 minutes exercising at the gymnasium four times a week, these small goals are much more likely to be achieved.

Some people's procrastination is based on unrealistic big promises they make to themselves about how much work, study or practice they will do today, tonight, or this week, when the reality is that they have done virtually nothing for months. If you have been seriously wanting to work, but have done very little for a long time, how confident will you be that you can meet such big self-promises? I (RWF) have treated non-studying students who, at the start of every evening, promise themselves that tonight they are really going to get into it and do five or six hours of hard work. Despite their repeated experience of multiple failures in carrying out this promise, they keep on making it. Of course it makes sense for them to try to study when the task is so great, but it makes no sense for them to keep making such transparently unrealistic promises to themselves. In such a situation, the thing to do is to reduce the promise to 10 or 15 minutes of study, for the first night's quota, and to increase the commitment over subsequent nights. What happens is that the student will probably do the 10 minutes because it isn't much, will feel good about that, will probably do another 10 minutes, and so on. What starts off as a 10-minute effort might grow into an hour or more of study on the first night. This is a can't-lose deal. To undertake to do 10 minutes of study is not humiliating; what is humiliating is to make and break so many promises and to act ineffectually and irresponsibly over several months.

If you are like those non-studying students, but are reluctant to try the 10-minute method, ask yourself why. Are you thinking that you should not set yourself such a childishly small task? If you are, start disputing the 'should' — ask yourself, 'Where is it written that I should not?'

14 Relaxation Methods

It is not possible to be free of muscle tension (that is, relaxed) in your body and at the same time experience anxiety (McKay, Davis and Fanning: 1997). Hence therapeutic relaxation (distinct from the relaxation of watching television, reading, walking, and so on) can be a significant tool in your repertoire of skills for dealing with the stress of performance challenges.

Here we describe two methods of rapid relaxation. Try both, and choose one to learn and practise. Rapid relaxation is applied to counteract rising or excessive arousal. Long relaxation sessions make you feel good at the time, but they are of little use in stressful situations. There is also self-hypnosis, which has a different application.

Record your anxiety levels

You need to know what is happening to your body when you are anxious. Remember the SUDS diary (Chapter 2). Refer to the records you made, or, better still, resume keeping the diary.

In order to keep an accurate stress diary, spend a few minutes every night reviewing the day and making as many entries as you need. Keep reminding yourself that you are taking a significant step towards controlling your performance anxiety by becoming very sensitive to your body's distress signals. You will soon have the tools to help.

Most importantly, commit yourself firmly to practising your relaxation exercise whichever one you may be working on, every day. When you practise, be where you are unlikely to be disturbed, silence the telephone, and sit in a comfortable armchair.

1. The meditation-relaxation technique

Some people learn this technique quickly, and you may find it helpful if you have a performance challenge soon.

- Allow 10 to 20 minutes, preferably at the same time each day. Choose a time not soon after heavy exercise or any hectic activity.
- Sit in a comfortable chair, preferably one that supports your head. You need to be relatively upright, in order to maintain concentration and wakefulness.
- Sit comfortably, with feet flat on the floor, and hands apart.
- Allow half a minute or so to slow your breathing, then focus on your abdomen, how it moves, and how it feels as it moves.
- Each time you breathe in, feel your abdomen move out, and silently count the breath. Count in cycles of 10 breaths.
- Breathe out slowly, making your breaths in and out of about equal length.
- The instant before breathing out, silently say 'relax' or 'calm' or 'easy' or 'let go'. Stay with the word or words you prefer, saying it each time.
- As you breathe out, feel your abdomen and your whole body — your limbs, neck, throat, jaw, eyes and forehead — relax.

Relax like this for 10 to 20 minutes. If your mind wanders, accept that this has happened, and return to the task. You cannot make yourself relax. What you are doing is establishing the conditions in which you can allow yourself to relax.

Keep a record of your relaxing, and its effects. At the end of each session, note on a 10-point scale how well you relaxed, where 10 = total relaxation. In your first sessions you will achieve probably only two or three points. That's fine.

At least ten times a day, pause, take three relaxing breaths (using the above breathing technique), and do the count-and-relax technique. When you can, repeat this several times.

Nothing much will happen at first, but you will become better at it. If you need to be reminded to do these quick relaxations:

> (a) carry a timer that squeaks to remind you, or
>
> (b) stick about eight red dots (available from stationers) around your environment — on your watch, your wallet, the telephone, your car's steering wheel, the refrigerator, and so on. Each time you see one, do a three-breath relaxation. Don't exceed this number of dots; if you do, they will become so familiar you will not notice them, or
>
> (c) record each time you relax by marking a card, or with a golfer's counter, or on a knitter's row counter. Self-monitoring makes you more aware of what you have to do. Each night, record the estimated number of times that you relaxed, and the effect (0–10 scale).

Also, whenever you feel anxious or otherwise disturbed, practise the 10-minute relaxation exercise described above, and note any fall in your SUDS (Subjective Units of Discomfort — see Chapter 2).

2. Isometric relaxation

Isometric relaxation is different. Many of its exercises do not involve any apparent movement or change in posture, so they can be done any time, and often. In time, you may find yourself doing them without thinking, automatically keeping muscular tension to a minimum. You will be able to use these exercises working at your desk, waiting for the traffic lights to change, or standing in a queue, for example.

When you practise isometric relaxing:

- breathe in gently (using diaphragmatic/abdominal breathing), hold the breath for about seven seconds, and at the same time gently tense various muscles (see below);
- after about seven seconds, gently breathe out, think 'relax', and slowly — take about seven seconds — release the tension from your muscles;
- concentrate on inhaling and exhaling gently, and on tensing and relaxing your muscles, and not on precise timing;
- then close your eyes, and for one minute breathe calmly, and each time you exhale, think 'relax', and let the tension flow from your muscles.

■ afterwards, take a short time to enjoy thinking of how these muscle groups feel relaxed and comfortable, and perhaps warm.

Remember, isometric exercises are intended to be a gentle method of relaxing, so do not tense muscles too much or too quickly.

There are various isometric tensing exercises. These examples are suggestions that we assume you will modify and add to, according to your requirements. In each instance, follow the routine described above, and vary the muscle groups that you tense, according to the circumstances or your particular needs.

1. When you are alone, sitting or lying down, tense your legs and arms by holding them straight, with your hands clenched, and make your whole body tight. Don't forget all the muscles from your neck to your scalp.

2. When sitting, tense your legs, using one of these methods. lock your ankles together and try to separate your legs, or pull the upper one down and back, with the lower one resisting, or press your ankles together with your knees apart, or tuck your feet back and press your ankles outwards against the chair legs.

3. When standing, tense your legs by bracing your knees back and scrunching your feet, or pull them towards or away from each other.

4. Tense your arms, using one of the following methods. Clasp your hands in your lap, and slowly try to separate them. Rest your hands, one above the other in your lap. Press the upper hand down and the lower hand up. Reverse their positions sometimes. Place your hands under the seat of the chair or under your bottom and pull upwards. Push down or up against the edge of your desk. Feel the tension in the hands and arms.

   Devise other manoeuvres for your limbs.

5. Slowly and gently clench your teeth, tensing the jaw muscles.

   Try to include and/or devise isometric relaxation exercises that could be particularly useful to you. For instance, if your shoulders are often tense, draw your shoulders up and forwards and tighten your neck, or if you get headaches, raise your eyebrows and forehead, or frown.

Self-hypnosis and auto-suggestion

Self-hypnosis can be very useful. It is an easy and efficient way for you to learn to relax, if, like 9 out of 10 people, you are hypnotisable. The advantages of light hypnosis are that you may relax more readily, in order to learn a rapid relaxation technique, and increased receptiveness to suggestions can considerably enhance methods that require visualisation, such as Rational-Emotive Imagery (REI) and self-instructional training (SIT), described in the next chapter.

Hypnosis defined

Hypnosis is an altered state of attention and awareness (not consciousness) that results from focusing the mind on some suggestions, and allowing oneself to be receptive to those suggestions.

The depth or intensity of the hypnotic state can vary considerably. For your purposes, the light trance of self-hypnosis is all you need.

Hypnosis — myths and facts

1. Hypnosis is not sleep. The hypnotised subject commonly finds that he can be alert and aware, or drowsy and detached. Either way, he is always as responsive to his surroundings as he needs to be. If he smells smoke and hears the crackle of flames, he may even beat the hypnotist to the exit.
2. On entering the state of hypnosis, the subject definitely does not lose control of himself. Think of the hypnotised subject as being relaxed, but always able to stop the self-hypnosis session at any time. When a hypnotic subject on the stage is acting crazily, and is apparently controlled by the hypnotist, he is only doing what he wants to do (why else would he be there?), and the hypnotist is helping him. They are cooperating.
3. The hypnotic 'trance' is not a state projected onto a suggestible subject by a strong-willed hypnotist. We all have the potential to enter the hypnotic state to a greater or lesser degree, so 'strong' or 'weak' wills are irrelevant. Consider this: most of us slip into and out of hypnosis spontaneously from time to time without the help of a hypnotist or auto-hypnotic procedures. This happens when we are absorbed in daydreaming or

reading. So, in learning self-hypnosis, you will be enhancing and applying an ability you already possess, and in using it you will experience the enjoyable state of deep relaxation.

This brief exercise will introduce you to how hypnosis is induced and how it feels.

- Allow about 5 minutes.
- Sit comfortably, in a chair that supports you well.
- Let yourself go limp and loose.
- Think of your breathing; let it become slow and rhythmical. If that is not easy, forget it. Don't try to make anything happen — this is no time for performance anxiety.
- Think of your arms. Imagine that they are becoming heavy. Feel them pressing down into the arms of the chair.
- With each breath out, say 'heavy' to yourself, and imagine your arms becoming heavier and heavier.
- Imagine that your arms are so heavy that you cannot lift them, no matter how hard you try.
  If you respond positively, you may notice that:
- Your arms feel heavy, even if you can lift them;
- You become comfortable and relaxed, and reluctant to move;
- You temporarily put aside, to some extent, the active control you normally have over your thoughts and behaviour.
- At the end of the trial, tell yourself to be alert, free to move, and relaxed.

You can conclude that you hypnotised yourself and suffered no ill effects. If you think it was too easy for it to be 'real' hypnosis, you are confusing the reality with the popular stereotype. Your goal is to learn how to achieve the lightest state of hypnosis necessary to facilitate relaxation and auto-suggestion. And that's all.

Before we begin, here are some general guidelines.

1. Don't try too hard. In fact, don't try at all. Just relax, tune out the world around you for a short while, and listen carefully to the instructions you give yourself.
2. Resist asking yourself, 'Am I hypnotised now?'. You may do so once or twice, but don't pester yourself. If you feel relaxed, calm, and reluctant (but able) to move, then you have probably entered a very light trance, which is all you need, so be content with it.

Self-hypnosis instructions — eye-fixation induction method
First, remember that you can end the proceedings at any time, simply by wanting to, by telling yourself, 'Wake up', or by counting from five down to one.

1. Sit in a comfortable chair with head support, and settle into it.
2. Look upwards, so that you feel a slight strain in your eyes, and find a spot to stare at. Let your eyes blink as much as they want to.
3. Silently tell yourself that your eyelids will begin to feel heavier and heavier as you gaze at the spot, and that although you easily could keep your eyes open, you will soon realise that you will feel more comfortable when you allow them to close.
4. Tell yourself over and over that when you allow your eyes to close you will enter a state of relaxation, while remaining aware of everything around you.
5. Close your eyes when they feel a bit heavy or you feel ready to do so, and take in a deep, slow breath. Hold it for 5 to 10 seconds, then slowly breathe out.
6. As your lungs and chest relax, let the relaxation spread through your body. Let your breathing become slow and comfortable.
7. Each time you exhale, say the word 'relax' to yourself. Imagine that each time you exhale you are breathing out tension. After a few minutes you will feel relaxed, calm and comfortable.
8. Imagine that your body is becoming heavy. Focus on the feeling of heaviness.
9. Concentrate on each major muscle group of your body — one by one, in the following way:

STAGE 1
Keep your breathing slow and easy. Exhale as slowly as you inhale, and be aware of your abdomen letting go as you breathe out. Each time you breathe out, think of a part of your body, and silently say, 'Warm and heavy'. Linger on each part for a few breaths before moving on.
Follow this sequence:
- Tell yourself that your forearms are becoming loose and warm, and heavier and heavier.
  Think of your upper arms, and do the same with them.

- Then do the same with your shoulders, throat, tongue, lips, cheeks, eye muscles, forehead, neck, chest, abdomen, back muscles, buttocks, thighs and calves.

     When you have completed this you will feel calm, peaceful and relaxed.
- Deepen the trance by thinking the word 'deeper' as you exhale. Do this several times.
- Now imagine yourself at the top of a slow-moving escalator that is going down, or a long staircase. Start your descent, and as you slowly move downwards, silently say the word 'deeper' and feel yourself letting go, allowing yourself to sink further into a comfortable and safe trance. Continue the trance-deepening journey downwards for as long as you wish, but remember that you need only achieve a light trance.

STAGE 2
When you feel that you have reached a good level of relaxation (or a light hypnotic trance), then it is time to work on a visualisation method, such as REI or SIT, or to give yourself suggestions (See Chapter 15).

STAGE 3
When you are ready to leave the trance and resume your routine, all you need do is say, 'Come out of the trance. Count from one to five and my eyes will open. I will feel refreshed and relaxed.'

     Repeat this exercise daily to ensure that you experience regular, deep, mind and body relaxation, and most importantly, that your SIT coping statements are thoroughly installed in your thinking about your performance/challenge.

     A session of self-hypnosis should last for about 10 to 20 minutes.

Exercises and Techniques

Gaining emotional insight

Often in therapy, a person gains an understanding of the nature of their irrational beliefs, and can see these are not factual, and are internally inconsistent, illogical and self-defeating. He or she can see how rational beliefs and philosophies are better in every way, and how adopting them will help him or her to feel act and perform smarter and better.

Inconveniently, it does not always work out this way. Instead of enlightened change, to a good life of rational feelings and behaviours, negative emotions and behaviours can arise when one is confronted with difficult performance challenges and other anxiety-provoking situations. So a person may try and confront his fears, but this can lead to emotions that are too strong, and the attempt fails.

Take heart. This is actually a stage in the acquisition of rational beliefs and philosophies, when a person has achieved intellectual insight, but insufficient emotional insight. Emotional insight is achieved, when, for example, you *know* that someone's opinion of you is merely that — an opinion — and you are minimally, or not at all, disturbed by this. You know that nothing can measure or change what you are, and you believe it. Believing it, you can act upon it by speaking up if that is appropriate, by taking sensible risks, and feeling, behaving and performing with confidence.

Acquiring emotional insight usually doesn't happen in a wonderful flash. It has to be worked at, by doing reading, writing, imagery and behavioural exercises. Here are 11 exercises that you will probably find helpful.

1. Rational-Emotive Imagery — negative type

This technique was devised by Dr. M.C. Maultsby, and is an exceedingly useful technique — it is actually indispensable. It can be used for preparing oneself for future feared events, or for coming to terms with past ones. Let's say, for example, that you are scheduled to give a talk to 20 or 30 people, and that you feel afraid when you think about it.

To do REI will probably take about two minutes, but you should allow five minutes the first time.

- Sit comfortably, close your eyes, and picture the feared scene. Concentrate, and make the scene as vivid as you can, putting in all the details you can think of. When the scene is fully developed, note how you feel; presumably afraid and extremely anxious.
- Now briefly ask what your self-talk is. It will be irrational, and intense enough to account for why you feel the way you do.
- Now keep the scene as it is, and do not change it in any way.
- Focus on your anxious feelings.
- Now make yourself, let yourself, reduce your anxiety, until all you feel is concern, and certainly not fear.
- You may get this concerned feeling for only a moment, but as soon as you do, open your eyes and ask what is your self-talk now. You will find it is rational, perhaps something like 'I have prepared well, and I can probably hold most people's interest. Even if some of them don't like it, I will hardly be burnt at the stake.'

Note that the A (activating event), has remained unchanged, and that the focus is on the C (consequence). In order for the C to change, the B (self-talk) must change. Effective rational Bs are not grandiose, and there is no suggestion of mastery of the situation; it is simply coping.

For REI to be effective, it must be performed 20, 30 or 40 times, not all at once. Do it for a couple of minutes, two or three times a day. It may be more practical for you to practise REI, repeatedly for 10 minutes once a day.

Some people find it useful to induce hypnosis and/or relaxation before doing REI, as it enhances visualisation and the sense of involvement. You might try this.

2. Rational-Emotive Imagery — positive type

In this version of REI you visualise the same scene, but this time it is essential that you perceive yourself as coping, that you feel reasonably calm, no more than concerned, concentrating on speaking thoughtfully and clearly, emphasising points, making eye contact with members of the audience, and generally performing in a way that is acceptable, if not ideal.

Stay with this imagery, and let it become fully established. When it is, ask what your self-talk is, and it will be rational, as in the previous example.

All the comments about practising negative REI apply to positive REI.

REI, and some of the other techniques, can be used in a graded fashion. Staying with the example of giving a talk, you could first do REI for giving a talk with nothing going wrong.

When repeated practice gets you to the point where the imagery no longer causes any irrational emotions, change the A to make it more confronting, such as having a member of the audience looking bored or irritated, falling asleep or leaving early, or your being unable to answer a question, or your hands shaking, or making mistakes.

We'd better state the obvious by pointing out that improving your feelings in imagery is not an end in itself; the effect transfers to the real-life situation.

3. The blow-up technique

This technique helps to bring your fears down to size by first inflating them to ridiculous proportions.

Picture yourself giving the talk, and having something go wrong, so that your audience is displeased. It is worse than that; they are uncontrollably enraged. A riot breaks out, chairs are thrown, rotten fruit is pitched at you. A lynch mob forms. You narrowly escape, and are whisked away, huddled in the back of a car. Within hours the streets fill with rampaging, howling mobs, incited to violence by your crummy speech. You watch the evening news on television, and naturally, there you are, blamed for this civil unrest. You are distracted from the television by the sound of gunfire and explosions. The sky is lit up by numerous burning buildings. You know that you are entirely to blame for this horrifying state of affairs. A state of emergency is declared, and you, because of your deplorable public-speaking skills, have to flee the country. But wherever you go, for the rest of your life, you are reviled and rejected, as rotten public speakers should be. You spend the rest of your days in a remote, primitive community, your hair matted with filth, dressed in rags, and begging for scraps of food. You have plenty of time to reflect on the fact that if you had given your talk calmly and competently, none of this would have happened.

Repeat this exercise often, until it helps you to truly appreciate that the thing you fear, giving a speech and perhaps boring or displeasing a couple of people, or even quite a few people, in one audience, does not amount to much in the grand scheme of things.

4. Attacking your critic

Many of us have a loud, critical, inner voice. Most of us are all too familiar with this voice, the critic, because we hear it often, especially when we have a performance challenge on our minds. At these times, it mercilessly seeks out our weak points, exaggerating and carping on about them when we are usually at our most vulnerable.

It sets unattainably high standards for us to achieve, and when we cannot meet them, abuses us with such names as 'failure' and 'idiot'. Too often, we believe its lies. If we let it, the critic will erode our confidence and self-acceptance, and, at the very least, diminish the robust energy we need to initiate and sustain new ventures and projects.

Why do we keep listening?

If we continue to listen, we do so because the critic actually seems to help us at times (McKay and Fanning: 1987). Occasionally the critic will goad us to work and work at something, so we actually achieve our goal, but at a whopping psychological and perhaps physical price. But we achieve, and the critic is silent for a short time while we bask in peace and pleasure. That's the trick. We think we achieved and feel so good because we listened to the critic's voice. What has happened, of course, is that if we have succeeded, we have done so despite the critic's interfering and anxiety-provoking harangues.

Internal monologue

Most of the time we are awake, we carry on an endless internal monologue with ourselves. We comment on Lucy's new dress, the state of the garden, the nation, anything. It's part of the 'stream of consciousness', which includes sensory impressions, images, stray thoughts and so on.

The critic's voice blends in with this monologue, making it indistinct and hard for us to recognise.

You may have heard the internal critic, the bully, the enemy, the nagger — whatever you want to call this voice — all your life, but perhaps you haven't thought of it as external to yourself, barging into your thoughts like a malevolent intruder. Some people find it helpful to think of their negative self-talk in this way, as they find it easier to strongly mentally clobber something outside themselves than to reason internally with themselves. The critic can more easily be thought of as alien, 'not the real me', 'a cruel bully' and so on, that can be silenced for short periods, then for longer and longer periods of time. In time, you may find that the critic's voice becomes fainter.

But be absolutely sure of this. If you wish to reduce the critic's attacks on you, and to eventually silence it, you must learn how to dispute the irrational beliefs (Chapters 6–12) that the critic activates. With some experience, you will probably learn to dispute convincingly and fast. If you lack these skills, the critic will certainly attack and harm you many times more often than it otherwise could. Your counter-attacks will be short-lived, and you will pay in the long term with prolonged suffering, perhaps ill health, and certainly no improvement in your performance anxiety.

What follows is a description of a simple technique for turning the attack back onto the critic, but bear this in mind: the critic is pretty obviously a deeply ingrained bad habit, your self-talk expressing negative irrational beliefs about yourself. If you have disputed these, you will then be better able to attack the critic effectively. It's like defeating the main army and then going after the lone sniper who does not know his side has lost the battle. But if you ignore the main army and only attack the sniper, you'll lose. Keeping that in mind, read on, and find out what to do about the critic.

Listen for your critic's voice

Listen to your internal monologue, and turn the spotlight on any item of criticism, nagging, abuse or self-slandering. These are your targets. Go after them. You would not talk to a good friend like this, so why on earth do it to yourself? Remember that your critic is skilled at spiking your ongoing internal monologue with put-downs. Listening for these psychological hits is the first thing you can do to protect yourself.

Example: I am having my first lesson with my new violin teacher this afternoon.

Critic: 'You've got no chance of pleasing your new teacher. Your violin is lousy. Anyway, she only works with talented musicians. Not people like you. You will only humiliate yourself. Don't even bother turning up.'

Usually, the critic does not talk to you like that. It is likely to use a shorthand method of put-downs such as 'New teacher → >horrified → > terrible violin → > no-talent → > humiliation! → > don't go!'

Example: After the dentist's appointment, you intend to pick up the paper and some groceries and go home.

Critic: 'Can you remember the groceries you want to buy? Bet you forget at least one item. You're too stupid to remember anything much.'

Critic shorthand: 'Buy groceries → > you → > forget something → > stupid! → > again!'

These examples may seem trivial, but if you are attacked by dozens of similar comments, day in and day out, it is easy to develop an uncomfortably low level of self-acceptance (usually referred to as low self-esteem).

See the critic's movie show

Sometimes the critic doesn't speak at all. Instead, just to vary things a bit, it re-runs movies of embarrassing or difficult moments that we wish we could forget, isolated disturbing scenes, flashes and snapshots.

Pangs of misery and stabs of anxiety

The critic can mess up some time in our day by sending us powerful nasty feelings. Take some time and think hard — what images and what critical self-talk can you find? They must be there — feelings do not just turn up.

After finding the self-talk, work at uncovering and disputing the basic irrational beliefs and philosophies that the critic is invoking — see Chapters 6 to 12. You may find the questionnaire in Chapter 19 to be helpful in this task.

Dealing with the critic

Because we have spent so much time listening to and reacting to the critic's voice, we believe it, and suffer, suffer, suffer. However, we can learn to turn the critic's voice way down, and eventually, right off. We can do this by attacking it (a) first at the time of the attack, and (b) later by learning how to comprehensively dispute the irrational beliefs underlying the critic's attacks. The Loop-Tape technique and other techniques described here can also be effective in warding off the critic's voice.

The blast-back treatment — the initial attack

Tune in to the babble inside your head, and listen for the critical voice that can so easily insinuate itself into the general chatter.

Once you have heard it, and have isolated some of its abuse: ('stupid', 'lazy', 'you shouldn't have to do this', 'get it right for once in your life', 'what will they think now?' and so on), shock the critic with a return blast (McKay and Fanning: 1987).

Don't try to politely ask the critic to leave you alone. That will not help you. Amuse yourself by thinking up the nastiest abuse you can muster, and scream it (inside your head) at the critic. Get stuck into it. This is war.

'Rack off, creep!'
'You have cost me too much for too long.'
'No more of your rubbish, no MORE!'
'Goodbye, liar!'

'Shut up, you !#%!!**^%!'

Your critic will be silenced — for a short while. Perhaps it falls back in surprise. After all, you may have rewarded your critic by being easily intimidated and believing its lies. Most of us do.

As a short-term measure, in an emergency, the blast-back technique will be effective and useful, even if you have not previously disputed and demolished the beliefs that underlie the critical comments.

Disputing — the lasting treatment

However, if you only blast-back, and never thoroughly dispute, you may have to keep blasting back forever. So don't cut corners, and don't slack off. As soon as you are able, dispute, dispute, dispute.

Nevertheless, your critic will probably never disappear entirely. But you can at least become skilled at using the tools to handle any of the critic's attacks, and keep it turned way down. It is likely to end up sounding pretty silly.

Note: We have been introduced to the concept of the critic and its relationship to self-acceptance through the book *Self-Esteem* (New Harbinger Publications, Oakland 1987), by Matthew and Judith McKay and Patrick Fanning. For those readers who wish to explore the concept of the critic and ways of dealing with it in detail, this book is highly recommended.

5. The loop-tape technique

Loop tapes are cassette tapes that play continuously. They are used for the outgoing message (OGM) in telephone answering machines. You may need to buy one from a shop that sells such equipment. They play for different lengths of time; three minutes is a good length.

Record on the tape what it is that you want to attack. It might be irrational philosophies and beliefs reflecting the need for approval, and global rating. This irrational thinking could be expressed as 'I must never be disapproved of by anybody for any reason at all. What people think of me is a reflection of my worth as a person, so if anybody dislikes me or rejects me, it means that I am a worthless person, not equal to others, inferior. When I give a talk I must please absolutely everybody with everything that I say. If I don't, they will conclude that I am hopeless, stupid, not worth bothering with, all of which is convincing evidence that I am an inferior person.' And so on.

Speak slowly, leave pauses, put in everything you can think of, embellish. If you dry up before the three minutes is up, start again, and keep on at it until the tape is full.

To use the tape, set aside 10 or 20 minutes, and let the tape deliver its message over and over. You attack what you hear in any rational way that you can think of. Talk over the recorded voice, interrupt, swamp it with your assertions that it is wrong, that it is talking rubbish. State the facts. Aggressively question the logic. Ask if it is helpful to think like this. Assert that it is not. Point out that whoever made this stuff up was wrong, and it must be so, simply because of being human. Above all, be emphatic, using whatever rough language you choose to, and make sure that you believe everything you say, even if only partially at first.

A variant of this technique is to use the loop-tape to practise attacking the critic. Instead of the tape containing irrational philosophies and beliefs, record on it the sort of things the critic says, which, as we have pointed out, is irrational, negative, self-critical and self-abusive self-talk. Rehearsing with the tape in this way will help you be more able to attack back assertively and vigorously when you hear your critical voice.

5a. Loop-tape technique — blowing up feared consequences

Refer to the blow-up technique (see page 132). Record your description of the scene on the loop tape, and listen to it until you are merely bored or irritated. This may take 45 minutes or more. With repetition, you reach this point faster and faster.

5b. Loop-tape technique — exposure and desensitising to fears

Another approach to dealing with your critical voice is to densensitise yourself to it. If you have gone through the process of identifying the beliefs that the critical voice refers to, disputed the beliefs and the associated negative self-talk, and evolved rational beliefs, but still the critical voice presses on, one way of dealing with it, instead of attacking it, is to simply let it rant on, and by exposing yourself to it, desensitise yourself to the sound of it, and the content. You may find it useful or necessary to insert statements about the context of the critical comments. For instance, 'I can see myself on the court, about to serve in the club championship semi-final, and I can hear "You shouldn't be here. You're not up to this. You're no good at it. You're only here because you're lucky. This is it. You'll be found out. You're going to make a fool of yourself. Should have backed out of this."' And so on. Fill up the tape with all the self-critical accusations that you can think of, and treat yourself to large doses of it, in the following way.

Allow two hours for the first few sessions, even though you may need only 40–50 minutes. Sit and listen to the loop-tape in a setting where there are absolutely no distractions. Do not read, watch television, have the radio going, or talk with anyone else. Just listen. Don't answer back. Just remember, you are listening to a lot of tripe. But you have unconsciously trained yourself to be upset by this nonsense, and you are aiming to break this response, by listening passively and developing indifference to it.

Have a pen and paper in front of you, and note the date. After the tape has played for a couple of minutes, record your SUDS. Do this every 15 minutes. Your SUDS will probably rise, and your aim is to just see it out, and wait for your SUDS to fall. It may be helpful to breathe slowly to relax yourself, but focus on what you hear, not on the relaxing. If rational thoughts come into your mind, do not choke them off — after all, they are a healthy response. Continue like this until your SUDS falls by at least two points. Do not quit, or give up while your SUDS is being kept up by the critical voice. Stick with it until your declining SUDS indicates that you are desensitising.

If you can, it would be better for you to draw a small graph, with your SUDS on the ascending axis, and time, in 15-minute segments, on the horizontal axis. Repeat the exercise two or three times a week, and you should see that the initial SUDS becomes lower, and the decline to the base line becomes much faster. So after several sessions, it becomes a small blip, or nothing at all. At this point, if you can still hear the critical voice, you can much more easily ignore it, and by doing so you will gradually extinguish it.

Note: Do not employ this technique unless you are sure that you have disputed thoroughly, you know what the rational beliefs are, and you truly believe that the critical voice is just a bad habit.

6. What would it cost me?

This disputing method is useful if intellectual insight has been achieved, and is solid, but emotional insight is an elusive goal. The real problem is that there are other irrational beliefs that have not been uncovered and disputed. It is these that are holding up the works. Fairly common examples are people with agoraphobia (fear of crowds and confined places), and social phobia, who express a belief that if they overcome their irrational fears, they will then start going into crowded places or acting sociably, and that this would be dangerous for them! It is obviously irrational to everyone else, but it is quite enough to stop them from putting their rational beliefs into action. The same thing can certainly apply to performance anxiety.

If you are in this situation, ask yourself, 'If I reject the irrational beliefs, and wholeheartedly embrace the new rational beliefs, what would it cost me?'. This may uncover previously unrecognised and unexpressed fears about what bad things might happen, or what it might mean for you, should you think rationally about performance, and perhaps act upon these beliefs. The uncovered beliefs need to be disputed in the usual manner.

7. Worry management

This worry management method — risk estimation — gives the potential worrier the chance to closely examine the worst possible consequences of the feared experience and prepare coping thoughts and strategies to deal with it.

Note: Using this method, the anxious worrier must only allow himself to problem-solve in a structured way, during some pre-determined time — say, for 30 minutes before dinner. When worrying thoughts form at other times, as soon as they are noticed, they should be moved quickly to one side. The worrier must then distract himself in some way, postponing the worrying until it can be dealt with systematically in the problem-solving session.

Feared event _____

Self-talk _____

Rate SUDS (1–10)
(See Chapter 2) _____

Rate probability of feared event (1–10) _____

Assuming the worst happens _____

Possible coping thoughts _____

Possible coping actions _____

Revised prediction of consequences _____

Re-rate SUDS (1–10) _____

Evidence against the worst possible outcome _____

Alternative outcomes _____

Re-rate SUDS (1–10) _____

Re-rate the probability of event (1–10) _____

The example
The following risk estimation example was done by Jane, a music pupil of mine (EMF) who was overly concerned about how she would perform in a maths test she had to do in a few days.

(Although this method of worry management rests on probabilities rather than facts, Jane, as you will see, ends up feeling much less concerned about the possibility of not doing well at the future maths test. But although she was relieved and stopped worrying about it for the moment, her fears of how she could cope if she always failed maths and other tests were not tackled. In order for Jane to lose her fears of failing, she will need to uncover the core belief(s) that is/are causing her grief now, and work at resolutely challenging it or them. Nevertheless, the risk estimation has been included because it can be particularly useful in alleviating worry in the short term.)

Feared event: Failing or just passing my maths test

Self-talk: I am really scared about not doing well on the maths test and upsetting my parents!!

SUDS (1–10): 7

Assuming the worst happens (the worst possible consequences): I will be really, really disappointed about upsetting my parents. (Here, Jane sneaks in an 'and that would be awful!' because while disappointment is a rational, mild emotion, she was not responding mildly and rationally to the thought of failing, or just passing, the maths test.)

Possible coping thoughts: The maths test is only one of the tests I will be doing. There are other subjects in which I could do well and please my parents. My parents know how hard I try at everything I do. I can't do better than that.

Possible coping actions: I could study even harder and then I would know I really had done my best.

Revised predictions of consequences: I will probably do okay even if it's not to the standard that my parents (and I) would like. There will be plenty of opportunities for me to do well in all sorts of tests before I finish being a student.

Re-rate SUDS (1–10): 4

Evidence against the worst possible outcome: I've worked hard for this test, and so I'm likely to do okay, even if the result is not brilliant.

Alternative outcomes: I might do well and please myself and my parents. But if I don't, I can just knuckle down to working harder. My teacher could give me some extra work to do on the parts I find hard to do.

Re-rate SUDS (1–10): 4

Probability of the feared event (1–10): 3

As you can see, Jane, during her problem-solving time, found that she was able to calm herself by examining her fears in a systematic way, and coming up with alternative ways of thinking and behaving. She was able to quickly reduce her SUDS from an uncomfortable level of 7 to a reasonable 4.

This risk-assessment exercise, while not challenging the core irrational beliefs, provides convincing temporary relief for Jane and others whom I have seen use the strategy. Perhaps later, Jane, and others like her, will learn about and use the REBT techniques that make long-term relief from emotional disturbance more likely.

8. Behavioural exercises

Performance anxiety is overcome when you are able to do what you have been afraid of doing, with nothing more than minimal disturbance before or during the event. Behavioural exercises are essential in order to cement what you have learned, to help you develop emotional insight, and to help you recognise and overcome practical difficulties. In general, the exercises are known as risk-taking exercises. Let us emphasise that the risk refers only to the risks of normal living, striving and competing. There is no actual danger. It means making yourself repeatedly do what you have been avoiding, or doing too anxiously. Before, during and after each effort, focus on your thinking, and work hard at making it rational.

If possible, do just what it is that you have been anxious about, such as competing, performing, giving a talk, or whatever. But perhaps you will have to focus on your particular irrational belief.

- If you need approval, do inoffensive things that you believe others might tut-tut over.
- If you absolutely must succeed at something, make mistakes, in matters where mistakes are unimportant.
- If you believe that the world must be nice to you, and you must never suffer delay, inconvenience or discomfort, make yourself wait for things. Delay gratification. Make yourself uncomfortable. Do things on the computer that you know are likely to lead to frustration.
- If you think some merely dislikeable and unenjoyable experiences are awful and that you can't stand them, make yourself stand them, and while doing so, remind yourself that while you don't like it, it's not awful and you can stand it.
- If you are a keen global rater of other people, seek out someone whom you regard as totally boring or stupid. Spend some time with them, and see what you can do to draw out

some acceptable behaviour from them. Whenever you find yourself enthusiastically totally praising or damning an activity, a person or an object, try to re-express your dislike or preference in a more analytical way.

Make the challenges as big as you can cope with, but if any one of them is too daunting, break it down into smaller steps. A graded approach may take longer, but it may make it more likely that you reach your goal.

9. Mental imagery

There is nothing new about mental imagery. Most of us have been doing it, rehearsing a wide variety of situations, for most of our lives. It is this versatility that is one of the technique's strengths.

Mental imagery or mental rehearsal can help us with almost any performance challenge. Asserting yourself with a friend, neighbour or shop assistant, going to a party, asking someone out on a date, giving a speech at a family or business function, sporting challenges of any kind, music performance anxiety and any performance challenge you can think of, can first be experienced through mental imagery.

We use it often, almost automatically, because it gives us a chance to mentally cope with a problem or event before we have to confront it. If the situation is particularly bothersome or demanding, we have a chance of developing some confidence in our ability to deal with it in a more relaxed and capable way than we otherwise would. After all, if the performance challenge is difficult enough, we will tend to rehearse it mentally many times, so that when the performance situation arises in real life, we are more likely to feel familiar with many aspects of the situation. We have 'been there' lots of times.

The more significant the performance is to you, the more time and effort you will need to put in to achieve the results this technique can deliver, and they are considerable.

Terry Orlick, Olympic coach and author of *The Pursuit of Excellence*, describes the performances of Olympic athletes who take mental imagery so seriously that they practise it daily.

Eventually, when their imagery skills are well enough developed, they put aside as long as it takes, in real time, to mentally rehearse specific routines such as diving, skating, shooting basketball goals and difficult aspects of other sports. His accounts of various athletes' experiences with mental imagery are impressive.

I (EMF) have always mentally rehearsed piano pieces that I have been working on. I did not go nearly far enough in the imagery, in that I only rehearsed memorising the work. But still, since that was my only aim, it worked well enough. I would 'play' my piece by slightly moving my fingers on the steering wheel of the car, or on a table edge or any surface at all. Once I devised a new (and better) fingering for a difficult trill in a Mozart sonata as I walked down a street, immediately before I was to perform that sonata at a state conservatorium concert. I did not have the time or chance to try out the new fingering. I played it anyway, and it worked beautifully. I wasn't at all surprised. And since I was then still in the grip of performance anxiety, surprise would not have been unexpected.

Recognising the power of imagery, I advise senior music students who are highly motivated to perform well, and to do so with rational confidence, to mentally rehearse in real time, including in the imagery, such things as:

■ the feel of the piano bench and the pedals;
■ the atmosphere of the performance room;
■ scanning the body for tension and releasing it as soon as possible;
■ repeating a passage which included an error, and feeling satisfied about having played it better the second (or third) time through;
■ hearing the sound of the work they are playing, enjoying it, and being aware that others are probably enjoying it too;
■ anything they can think of to make the mental imagery as real to them as possible.

My example is music performance, but of course it can be varied in any way that is right for your performance, whatever that may be.

10. The cost/benefit analysis and the hedonic calculus

These strategies are to help clarify your rational and irrational reasons for behaving or thinking in self-enhancing and self-defeating ways. They are included in Chapter 13, in relation to procrastination. Readers are advised to read about it there (pp.112–121), before modifying the cost/benefit analysis and/or hedonic calculus, to make it relevant to other rBs and iBs and their associated behaviours.

As mentioned in Chapter 13, a cost/benefit analysis consists of drawing two columns. In one column list the advantages of taking a particular action, and in the second column, the disadvantages of taking that action. This exercise can help clarify the issues concerning a particular matter, and help in making a

A Advantages of accepting this task	B Disadvantages of accepting this task	C Advantages of not accepting this task	D Disadvantages of not accepting this task
1. The other women in the club will see that I am contributing. 2. I have not done any catering before, so I would learn about it. 3. I will be publicly thanked, and I will feel very proud of myself. 4. Doing this will help me to get to know other members.	1. Organising the food for a occasion of this size will be hard and I could mess it up. The other members would not be impressed. 2. I won't have a chance to play bowls on that day.	1. I will not have to worry about whether or not the food is all right, and just enjoy the day. 2. I won't have to do all the necessary work that catering for this occasion would entail.	1. I would not feel good about someone else doing it, now that I have been asked to do it first. 2. I would forgo the opportunity of learning a new skill and perhaps doing a good job of it. 3. I would miss an opportunity to get to know other club members.

Fig 15.1 *Hedonic calculus*

rational decision about it. The hedonic calculus is a more detailed version of the cost/benefit exercise.

Hedonic calculus
Situation: I have been asked to organise a committee to provide morning and afternoon tea and lunch for a 'Gala Club Day' for a visiting group of interstate bowlers. I am new to the club, and I want to make a good impression on the other members.

11. Self-instructional training

Self-instructional training (SIT) is based on the work of psychologist Donald Meichenbaum, the founder of one school of cognitive behaviour therapy. He devised the technique known as Stress Inoculation.

SIT is a very powerful technique. We have used it as a centrally important technique in treating examination candidates and other performance anxiety sufferers, and also taught a variation of the SIT technique to children and young people to help them manage their music performance anxiety. Almost all of them have reported later that it was the most effective technique in the treatment of their performance anxiety. In saying that, they were almost right. SIT is certainly very striking in its effects, but it has to rest on a solid foundation of REBT. If the old irrational beliefs are first demolished, then the new rational beliefs will find it much easier to gain a firm foothold.

The purpose of SIT is to train you to have rational self-talk in situations where you find it hard to do so. People often report that 'I really believe rational beliefs, but when I'm in the performance situation I am as irrational as ever.' This can happen at any time, particularly when a person is feeling overwhelmed by anxiety. SIT plants rational thoughts in your mind, so that when you are thinking about, approaching, or in, different stages of the performance situation, cognitive buttons are pressed, and you automatically think your well-rehearsed rational self-talk.

People report different experiences. Some say that they just found themselves calmly thinking their rehearsed rational thoughts. Others say that they could hear a cool rational voice in their head reciting the rational thoughts they had practised.

Importantly, either way, they felt strongly convinced of the truth of their thinking.

An outline of the principle and the method
1. First, you relax yourself, in order to:
- increase your capacity for visualising clearly, and
- maximise your capacity for accepting suggestions that you give yourself using any of the relaxing techniques in this chapter, but I (RWF) have found that self-hypnosis and auto-suggestion are often the most effective methods to use in relation to Self-Instruction Training.

2. Next,
- Imagine yourself in various stages of a performance situation. These stages are progressive, starting well before the event, working through the event, and continuing after it.
- At each stage, you rehearse, over and over, sets of rational, coping statements which you have previously prepared. These self-statements become attached to the scene, and later on, in real situations that resemble the ones that you have rehearsed, these statements are recalled so vividly that they are experienced as one's own thoughts — which, of course, they are.

Note: There is a parallel between the mental rehearsals of musicians and athletes.

The technique
Relax as much as possible using either self-hypnosis or the meditation-relaxation technique (Chapter 14).

You need to prepare sets of self-statements. See the examples later in this chapter. There are some criteria for these. There should be one to four statements for each stage, and they must:
- be brief, from one word to one line;
- be rational;
- be realistic and believable;
- be relevant;
- remind you to concentrate on the task;
- emphasise coping (not mastery);
- remind you of your strengths;
- remind you to acknowledge and accept discomfort and anxiety;

- remind you to scan for discomfort and to relax;
- remind you to monitor and accept difficulties and problems;
- emphasise positive feelings and positive outcomes.

They must avoid:

- denying discomfort and problems;
- grandiosity;
- any grandiose talk of mastery.

It is better to use positive language, such as 'I will stay in control (of my feelings)' rather than 'I will not panic.' You may also find it helpful to use strong and forceful language, including profanity, if that is your style.

Prepare sets of self-statements for these stages and events that include:

- any time in the weeks or months before, until the last minutes before, the performance challenge;
- the moments immediately before the challenge;
- just starting a performance, with no apparent problems;
- getting under way, with no apparent problems;
- confronting a problem, such as:
    (i)   being aware of an impending difficult patch;
    (ii) a moment of mediocre performance;
    (iii) being aware of anxiety symptoms;
    (iv) feeling overwhelmed;
    (v)   having just coped with a problem.

(As you can see, this deals with general problems that arise in most performances. Later in the chapter, we will address ourselves to specific situations and problems that occur in specific performance challenges.)

For some challenges it may be necessary to take a hierarchical approach, that is, to do a series of performance-challenge episodes, starting with easy situations and working up to the most difficult ones. For example, with public speaking anxiety, it may be necessary to start with visualising oneself practising alone, then to do a scene with oneself doing a trial run in front of family, perhaps four or five stages from the easiest up to the main event.

Example — student taking an oral examination

(The student is well prepared, naturally)

Stage 1 At any time before the exam, thinking about the exam. What is needed here is self-talk that is not depressing or anxiety-provoking:
1. I've worked hard, and I know my stuff so I'll probably do all right or even well.
2. Remember to relax; I don't have to be afraid.
3. I'll focus on the task.

Stage 2 In the last minutes before the exam:
1. Here's my moment. I can handle this and do well.
2. The examiners are not my enemies — they want me to succeed.
3. I'll watch my SUDS and relax.
4. Focus on the task.

Stage 3 Getting started:
1. OK so far.
2. I can cope with whatever happens.
3. Accept any tension and stay with the task.
4. I can keep this up.
5. I'm doing all right (at any stage).

Stage 4 Well into the examination:
1. I'm doing okay.
2. I can keep this up.
3. Stay focused.

Stage 5 Confronting a problem. There is a variety of problems and some are specific to particular activities.
A. Awareness of a difficulty ahead, such as a possible question about a shaky topic. The task here is to stay in the moment and not think about things that one can do nothing about at the time.
1. I'm doing okay.
2. Meet that one if it happens.
3. Stay in the moment and stay focused.
B. Being asked a difficult question. The examination candidate needs to control her feelings and think about the question and her answer.
1. Pause, think. What do they want?

2. I can handle this.
3. They are on my side.
4. Slow-breathe. Relax. Focus.

C. Concern that an examiner might be bored or hostile. How the examiner feels is his or her business, and nothing that the candidate can do anything about, so it is irrelevant.

1. That's his concern.
2. I can only control myself, so relax and focus.
3. Stay with the task, and get on with it.

D. A moment of mediocre performance. Time to accept that life is not perfect and neither is our candidate.

1. That bit wasn't so good. Tough!
2. I'm doing okay and that was just a moment.
3. It's gone, so move on and keep focused.

E. Awareness of anxiety symptoms. Time to remember control techniques.

1. I can handle this.
2. What's my SUDS?
3. Slow-breathe, relax and feel my SUDS fall.
4. Stay on the task, and focus.

Stage 6 The problem is past. It's time for a self-administered pat on the back, and to assert that this was a problem dealt with, and not a lucky escape.

1. That's good. I knew what to do and I did it.
2. I coped. I handled it well.

Stage 7 Getting close to the end. It is important to remain motivated and to maintain concentration.

1. Nearly there.
2. Stay on the ball and don't ease up.
3. Stay with it.

Stage 8 After the performance/challenge. Time for self-commendation and anti-awfulising.

1. I've done it.
2. I handled everything as well as I could. I coped.
3. That wasn't too bad at all.
4. Anxiety was not a problem.
5. I can do this any time.

Installing the self-instructions

When you have worked out what sets of self-statements you want to learn, and when to use them, the next step is to install these thoughts. Here are a couple of techniques to help you.

(NB. As mentioned earlier in this chapter, your coping statements will almost certainly be more effectively and efficiently installed if you relax before each SIT session with the meditation-relaxation technique or self-hypnosis).

Making an audio-tape

Record the self-statements onto an audio-tape and play them back to yourself. To do this, first describe the scene that you are working on. Leave a silence of 20 to 30 seconds to let the scene develop clearly and strongly, and then recite your self-statements. When you have worked through all the lines associated with that scene, move on to next. It could be something like this.

'I am working outside the exam room. Five minutes to go. Most of the students look nervous. The good students look calm and confident.' *Pause for 10–15 seconds, longer if necessary, to let the scene develop.* 'I think ...

- ... here's my moment. I can handle this and do well. *Pause for about 20 seconds.* 'They are not my enemies — they want me to succeed. Watch my SUDS and relax.' *Pause for about 20 seconds.*
- 'I am sitting and reading the questions, waiting for the signal to start.' *Pause for about 20 seconds.*
- I think 'Think about each question. What are they really asking?' *Pause for about 20 seconds.* 'I'll watch my SUDS and relax if I need to.' *Pause for about 20 seconds.* 'I've worked and I know my stuff. I can handle this.' *Pause for about 20 seconds.* 'Pace myself. Stay aware of the time.' *Pause for about 20 seconds.*
- 'I have been writing for several minutes. No problems.' I think 'I'm OK so far. I can cope with this. Stay cool and watch my SUDS.' *Pause for 20 seconds.*
- And so on.

You have to tailor this to your own responses. Some people can visualise a scene rapidly and vividly. Other people need more time to let the scene develop in their minds. You should practise trying to visualise the scene as clearly as you can. Some people need to concentrate on the self-instructions for only a few seconds in order to attach them to the scene. Most people need 20–30 seconds, and some need up to twice that long.

Experiment before you make the tape, and make your pauses of a length that suits you.

If you prefer to not voice-record your rational self-statements, write (or print) on successive numbered system cards or pages of an exercise book, the scene descriptions and some related self-instructions, keeping them easy to read, and use these as your prompts.

Learning the self-instructions

Sit quietly, and take as much time as you need to relax. To use the tape, have the recorder near you, and, disturbing yourself as little as possible, switch it on, listen, and follow the instructions.

To use the cards or book, put them or it on a cushion or tray on your lap so that you do not have to move your head in order to read the words. You want to be able to read by doing nothing more than opening your eyes. Turn the page or flick the card away as you progress.

When you visualise the scene, ensure that you put in enough detail — touch, taste, smell, any relevant sensation, in order to make the scene as vivid as possible. Recite the self-statements over and over again until they feel as though they belong in the scene. Then it is time to move on, to the next set.

Note: Whenever you say the word 'relax' to yourself, do exactly that — follow the instruction.

When you tell yourself to check your SUDS, do it.

As there is a very wide range of performance challenge situations that can cause anxiety, it follows that there are issues that are common to them all, as well as some aspects that are very individual. So some activities will require their own specific self-talk, which would be inappropriate in other situations. The requirements are very similar for people doing oral examinations, performing musicians, and someone making a speech. But tennis players, golfers, schoolteachers and dinner-party hosts will have different self-talk requirements. We cannot, in this book, cover every aspect of every performance challenge activity; all we can do is give you some examples and ideas, and express a belief in your ability to work out for yourself what you need to think at given stages and situations during your own particular performance challenges.

In the examples that follow, we are making some assumptions. These are that the candidate, contestant or performer knows his or her subject, has worked/trained/practised/rehearsed, and has a good knowledge of what strategies he or she wants to employ. This book is not about how to compensate for poor preparation.

Example: Giving a talk or lecture

1. Immediately before starting
I can do this.
I have rehearsed and I am well prepared.
They are on my side.
Slow-breathe, and relax.

2. Getting started
Pace yourself. Don't rush.
Focus on the topic.
Ignore distractions.

3. At any time, with no problems
I'm going well. I can keep this up.
Focus on the topic.

4. A problem occurs. For example, a slide is shown upside down or out of sequence, a verbal stumble is made or concentration momentarily lost
Big deal! I'm doing okay.
Pause, relax and think. Get back on track.

5. Someone looks bored or distracted
So what? No one can interest everyone.
I am doing okay. Ignore him, and focus on the task.

6. Becoming aware of anxiety symptoms
It's all right. I'm in control.
It can't hurt me, so I'll accept it.
Pause, relax, feel my SUDS fall and focus on the topic.

7. Having coped with the problem
That's good. I knew what to do, and I did it.
I handled it. I can do the same any time.

8. After the performance/challenge
That was good. I controlled my anxiety.
I stuck to my plan. I can do that again.

Example — A student preparing for and taking examinations

1. Weeks and months before
What must I do today?
I have my study plan.
I'll stick to my study plan and I'll be okay.
I don't have to worry. I'll just focus on today.
Relax and concentrate on the task.

2. Weeks and months before — feeling dispirited about the tedium of study
It is tedious but I can stand it.
I can last the distance, and I'll enjoy myself later.
It's a worthwhile goal, so I'll stick with it, and get what I want in the end.

3. Last days — revision time
I've worked hard, I know my stuff and I can do well.
I'll relax and stay calm enough.
I have my revision plan and I'll stick to it.

4. The last few hours before the exam
I can do this.
Watch my SUDS fall as I relax.
Slow-breathe, and relax.
I'll read the questions carefully and think before I write.

5. In the exam room reading the paper before starting the examination
Good. I can handle this.
Read carefully. Think about the questions. What are they asking?
Stick to my time schedule.
Slow-breathe and relax.

6. *Things are going well*
I'm doing well.
I feel excited — that's good.
Stay in control.
Focus on the task.

7. *Confronting a problem — a difficult question*
Pause, slow-breathe, relax and think.
I've done well so far, so keep this in perspective.
Just focus on the task.
Organise what I do know, and just get started.

8. *Another problem — feeling panicky*
My SUDS are up.
I can control this. Slow-breathe and relax.
Feel my SUDS fall.
Just focus on the task and again, think about what I do know.
Do what I did the last time and just get started.
I'll probably think of more things to write about as I go along.

9. *After the problems*
I knew what to do and I did it.
It worked and I can do the same again.
I'm in control (of me).

10. *After the exam*
That was good. My plan worked.
I knew what to do and I did it.
I stayed in control.
I handled it all well.
I can do the same again.

Example — A sports performance challenge
1. *Any time up to immediately before the event, thinking about it*
I'll accept any anxiety.
Anxiety happens, and I can stand it.
I will focus on the task.
I'll try hard, and I can handle whatever happens.

2. Immediately before the challenge
I can handle this.
All I can do is my best, and that's what I'll try for.
Ignore anxiety, and concentrate on the task.
One step at a time.

3. Early in the match
Things are going well.
I can keep this up.
Stay focused.

4. Problem — an error or bad patch
Big deal!
Let it go and get on with it.
It's only one slip.
I won't let it get to me.
Stay focused.
Stay in the moment.

5. Problem — being distracted by noise/onlookers
It doesn't matter.
Ignore it.
Focus on the task.
I can handle this.

6. Problem — feeling angry, perhaps seeing provocation
Don't get fussed about him/her.
It's his/her problem.
Being angry won't help.
Stay cool. Stay in control.
Focus on the task.

7. After dealing with the problem
That's good.
I handled it.
I knew what to do and I did it.
I can do the same again any time.

8. Towards the finish
You're not there yet.

Don't let go — stay with it.
Keep it up.
Stay focused, stay in the moment.

9. After winning
I stayed focused and played as well as I could.
Good.
I did my best and handled the anxiety.
Good. I enjoyed the match and I'm glad we won.

10. After losing
I stayed focused and played as well as I could.
That was good.
I wish I/we had won, but that's the way it goes.
I can stand not winning and still enjoy the sport.

Example — Pianist (performance or audition)

Stage 1 — Preparing for the performance
1. What do I need to do right now?
2. Work out a practice plan and stick to it.
3. Concentrate only on practising today's section and revising yesterday's work. That is the plan.
4. Silence the Critic. Yell.
5. I'm doing okay. The plan is working well.
6. I can revive this work on time if I keep this up.

Stage 2 — Confronting your anxiety immediately before the performance
1. I can meet this challenge well enough.
2. There is no need for fear.
3. Silence the Critic. I can do that.
4. Relax.
5. Breathe slowly.
6. I'm in control here.

Stage 3 — Getting started
1. Okay so far.
2. Stay focused.
3. I can keep this up.
4. I'm doing all right (at any stage).

Stage 4 — Well into the sonata
1. Not perfect, but it's good.
2. I can cope with whatever happens.
3. Stay focused.
4. I can keep this up.

Stage 5 — Making a mistake/ memory slip
1. Tough! That mistake doesn't have to throw me off — no big deal.
2. I can get the music score out if I want to — no big deal.
3. Back on track. Good.
4. Slow breath and relax.
5. Stay focused and think about the music.
6. I coped with the slip. Good.
7. Stay with it.

Stage 6 — Getting close to the end of the performance
1. Nearly through and I'm still doing okay.
2. Stay focused on the music.
3. Don't lose concentration.
4. I'm doing okay.

Stage 7 — After the performance
1. Not perfect, but it was okay, even quite good.
2. Despite a slip or two, I gave a musical performance.
3. Good on me. I coped well.
4. I coped with the anxiety.
5. I can do it any time.

These examples are to give you an idea of the sort of coping statements that could be helpful to you before, during and after a performance/challenge. Some of the incidents and stages will correspond with those points that you will need to prepare for, and some of the suggested statements will suit your requirements. But as you are an individual with your own particular strengths and weaknesses, stresses and challenges, you will almost certainly be better off generating your own coping statements for the various stages, using our suggestions as a guide only.

For a given situation you might think of six short phrases to learn, but when a challenge time comes, it may be that only one or two or three of them, or perhaps only one word, such as 'focus' will come to you. You can trust your mind to unconsciously choose what it needs to think for that particular occasion.

Returning to the examples' coping statements, read each one carefully, including those which appear to be quite irrelevant to your requirements. You may find something in our example statements that applies to you, or an idea may be planted in your mind that you can develop for the various stages of your performance challenges.

16 Clinical Conditions

As I (RWF) have discovered in clinical practice, there can be untreated psychological or psychiatric conditions underlying performance anxiety. These include:

■ depression;
■ anxiety disorders;
■ attention deficit hyperactivity disorder (ADHD).

I have known several performance anxiety patients whom it was necessary to treat for a mood or anxiety disorder. These are common conditions, but they are frequently not apparent to those who have them, or to doctors and psychologists.

A depressive or anxiety disorder will aggravate performance anxiety, and make it very much harder to treat. But there is good news: anxiety disorders and depression are treatable. The success rate, using psychological techniques and/or medication, is high. The psychological method most often used is cognitive behaviour therapy, which research has shown to be effective, as also is medication (see Chapter 17). Combined treatment with CBT and medication is the most efficient and effective.

This is not the place for a dissertation on illnesses, or a diagnostic or treatment service. All we can do is provide some information, and make some suggestions.

Consider thoughtfully the possibility that you have a depressive or anxiety disorder if:

- you definitely used not to have performance anxiety, and then it developed, and you don't know why;
- as well as having performance anxiety, you just don't feel 'right', you seem to have lost some of your spirit or verve, people say you have changed, and sometimes you don't understand your own reactions;
- you have a family history of any of these conditions.

Depression

Do not assume that because you are a healthy young(ish) person, or you don't cry or feel downright miserable, you cannot be depressed. Many people in their thirties and forties who believe they have been depressed for two years or so, realise, after they recover, that they had been depressed ever since childhood. Always feeling mildly or moderately depressed, they assumed that that was normal. Or, if they were ever aware that they were unhappy, they assumed that it was because of personal misfortunes or a 'weak character'.

If you are not depressed, you can say of yourself that:

- you are in good spirits, you are happy enough and you feel contented — for enough of the time;
- you think that life is definitely worth living;
- you are calm enough;
- you sleep well and wake refreshed;
- you have a good appetite, enjoy your meals and your weight is steady;
- you enjoy things the same as you always have;
- your interest in people and activities, and your energy, are normal for you;
- you consider yourself to be healthy (assuming that you are);
- you have not lost interest in sex.

But if you:

- feel down, flat or glum;
- think that life is pointless;
- consider your sleep unrefreshing, and it is delayed or broken or you wake early;
- are uninterested in food, and/or have lost weight;

- have poor energy and interest, tire easily, can't be bothered, can't get started or put things off;
- feel unwell, worry about aches and ailments;
- don't enjoy things as you used to, or are easily bored;
- feel anxious, irritable or angry, or rely on medicines or recreational drugs to calm you, and you don't know why;
- have lost interest in sex;

then consider the possibility that you are depressed.

Perhaps you have some depression symptoms, but don't think you are miserable. Some depressed individuals are irritable, sarcastic and critical, but their unhappiness is apparent only to others. You may think you could not possibly be depressed, because your life is running reasonably well, and you have 'nothing to be depressed about'. That does not matter. Depression is not a natural reaction to bad events, it is an illness.

This is not about the normal ups and downs of mood, which are brief and do not disrupt a person's life. Depression lasts for more than a couple of days, and it may recur, with patches of good mood, or it may grind on for years or decades.

Many depressed people function well (often less so in family and personal relationships than at work) and will say 'I am not miserable, and I don't feel like crying.' But when asked 'Can you say that you are happy and contented, and that you enjoy life?' they will reply 'Oh, God! Definitely not!'.

0____1____2____3____4____5____6____7____8____9____10
Unhappy   Flat   Blah   Getting by   Cheerful

Fig 16.1 *Mood rating scale*

If you think you may be depressed, self-observation is better than speculation, as always. Keep a record for one month. Each night, rate your mood, overall for the whole day, on the scale above. If over the month your mood rating is mostly 6 or less and rarely 7 or more, you may be depressed, and you had better seek professional advice. Many depressed people assume that the way they feel is a natural and inevitable response to their circumstances — family or love problems, lack of money, having to study, worrying about exams, competitions, contests and so on. If it were true that problems make depression inevitable, then almost everybody would be depressed, as almost everybody has problems. Misfortunes and setbacks make it harder, but not impossible, to be happy. No one can be happy all the time, but it is unhealthy to be too unhappy for too much of the time.

What can be done about depression?

- There are excellent CBT books, such as *Feeling Good* by Dr. David Burns, which provide self-treatment for mild and moderate depression.
- Two forms of brief psychotherapy for depression, CBT and Interpersonal Psychotherapy (IPT), have been shown to be effective. They are administered by psychiatrists and psychologists.
- Medication. Modern antidepressant drugs are safe, non-addictive, and usually effective. See Chapter 17.

If you think you may be depressed, you are probably right, so do something about it. Your task is to do the best that you can for yourself, so don't rationalise or procrastinate and don't be deflected or fobbed off by simple reassurances from well-meaning people, or inexpert advice from uninformed experts.

If you feel ashamed at the thought of not being in perfect mental health, and hate to admit to yourself that this may be so, then look for and dispute the beliefs that underlie this thinking. Do you have to be perfect in order to be good enough, or to have others approve of you? Would it be awful to need treatment, of any kind? Note the example of public figures who unashamedly tell how they have been treated for depression.

Remember this — treatment of any type must be effective, and it must last long enough, even if that means psychotherapy or medication for two years or more. It is your right to be happy, so try to ensure that you are. Too many cases of depression are treated too briefly and/or superficially, often because the patient pulls out early. This can lead to many years of unhappy and unfulfilled life, truly a sad consequence.

Depression and performance anxiety

Depression can cause performance anxiety directly, or make it worse if it was already present. This happens in several ways:

- Depression often causes generalised anxiety, so anxiety attacks are more likely, and more stressing. Resilience is lower, and episodes of performance anxiety are more disturbing and less controllable.

- Depressed people tend to overestimate the size of a task or challenge, and to underestimate their coping abilities. Negative thinking makes a person more ready to see situations as hopeless, and themselves as helpless.
- Depression reduces motivation and the ability to make an effort, and increases the likelihood of procrastinating. Depressed people are more easily discouraged, and inclined to give up too easily.

Even so, many depressed people manage to make a strong and consistent effort, and to function well at work, in their studies and in family life. They and others may not sense what they are going through.

Anxiety disorders

There are several anxiety disorders. People with these conditions tend to be anxious not only in the specific situations related to their condition, but generally. In a performance anxiety situation, they become anxious more easily, and have less control over how they think and feel.

Recovery from performance anxiety is quicker, more certain and more complete if a person is successfully treated for any concurrent anxiety disorder they might have. So, do recognise that anxiety disorders can happen to anyone, consider each of the conditions described here, and take the necessary rational and practical steps if you think you might have an anxiety disorder.

Social anxiety

Of the anxiety disorders, social anxiety (social phobia) is the most relevant to performance anxiety. Think of it as mega-shyness, far beyond what most people experience at various times in their lives. Small children are commonly shy with strangers, and many young adults are shy with their peers, especially with the opposite sex. Most lose their shyness as they mature, and it is generally regarded as not much of a problem. But for some it is much worse than that, and causes many years of fearing some or all social situations, severe anxiety in those situations, impoverished social life, and avoidance and limitation of friendships, romance, and study and work opportunities.

Social anxiety affects and afflicts all kinds of people, even the successful and prominent. Many famous performing artists and entertainers have led reclusive private lives because of social phobia.

The basis of social anxiety is fear of disapproval, of being thought stupid, boring, unintelligent, odd, bizarre, neurotic, unattractive or socially undesirable, and the further belief that this negative opinion is evidence that the person is no good. 'If Mr. X and Ms. Y, who hardly know me, think I am not worth knowing, then I must be (not worth knowing). Furthermore, if they observe my blushing/trembly voice/shaky hands/inability to eat or drink in company/stricken expression/extreme reticence/babbling they will have an excellent reason for condemning me.' In brief, it is a form of performance anxiety, in which the primary anxiety is based on the fear of negative evaluation.

Manifestations and effects of social anxiety

A small degree of social anxiety is common, and hardly a problem. Many people are uncomfortable, at least briefly, on entering a room full of strangers alone, or when being introduced to others, especially if the other person is of high status, very attractive or apparently very confident. But it is also normal to not dread these occasions, to confront them and to cope by tolerating the arousal and getting on with what has to be done. Social phobia can be general, occurring in all social situations except with the very closest of friends, or it can be highly specific to only one or two situations.

Consider the possibility that you have social phobia if you:

- dread any social interaction, such as talking to an attractive person, meeting strangers, formal gatherings, being conspicuous, being overheard, making phone calls, being criticised or talking to a superior;
- experience (and fear) blushing, shaky hands or voice, sweating, difficulty swallowing and/or other anxiety symptoms during, and possibly before, social situations;
- want to avoid any social situations because of anxiety.

Avoidance can be obvious, such as not attending, taking breaks outside or leaving early, or subtle, such as dressing drably so as to be inconspicuous, avoiding eye contact, talking softly, seeking low-lit areas, and making jokes to deflect the conversation from personal topics;

■ need to relax yourself with alcohol, medicines or recreational drugs before a social encounter.

Social phobia begins gradually, early in life. Without treatment it may improve very slowly, but for many people it is a life sentence. Its tendency to extinguish spontaneously is weak, for clear psychological reasons. If I dread disapproval, believing that even one person's poor opinion of me is evidence of my unworthiness, then I am never safe. If a hundred or a thousand consecutive people tell me what a fine chap I am, it should help to buck me up, but it can't ever give me a guarantee that the next person won't condemn me and buck me down again.

In someone with both performance anxiety and social phobia, the latter is the primary condition, so it must be the main focus of treatment. To ignore it, and to treat only the secondary condition, performance anxiety, would be largely a waste of time. Any improvement would probably be partial, and unstable. When the underlying social phobia is successfully treated, there is usually little or no residue of performance anxiety left to deal with.

Panic disorder

This condition is characterised by panic attacks and (for at least one month) fearing further attacks, worrying about possible harm such as dying in an attack, and changed behaviour related to the attacks.

A panic attack is not the same as feeling scared or running around, squawking. It is 5 to 10 minutes, but occasionally much more, of extreme anxiety, with physical symptoms such as shaking, sweating, palpitations, chest pain, feeling hot or cold, breathlessness, rapid breathing, dizziness, faintness and unreality feelings about oneself or the surroundings. The anxiety symptoms are misinterpreted by the victim as indicating that he is in imminent danger of dying, losing control, or going crazy. Understandably, this intensifies anxiety, so it rapidly spirals up to terror. This may happen several times a day, once or twice a week, or occasionally.

Many people have panic attacks rarely, perhaps one or two in a lifetime. Most of them recognise at the time that it's not an impending catastrophe, but anxiety, that is making them feel so bad, so they do not go on to develop panic disorder.

In a more benign form there are no full-on panic attacks; instead, there are mild and brief anxiety episodes consisting of two or three symptoms for a minute or two. These can be frequent.

The condition usually begins in early adulthood. The first panic attack is a very dramatic event, and is long remembered very clearly. It may have been precipitated by a shock, for instance the death of a friend, or a severe prolonged stress. It is often assumed at first that physical illness is causing the symptoms. This can lead to a desperate search for a non-existent medical condition, and terrified visits to hospital casualty departments in the middle of the night.

There are differences between panic disorder and social phobia, which do not matter here. To complicate things, some people have both conditions. Over 20 per cent of social phobia patients do; they have panic attacks in social situations or quite independently of any social anxiety.

Treatment
The most effective treatment for social phobia is cognitive behaviour therapy, with or without medication. With hard work, excellent results can be obtained in a few months, and even in a couple of weeks in some intensive group therapy programs. The task is to dispute the irrational beliefs that cause ego anxiety (the demand for acceptance, and global self-rating) and discomfort anxiety (awfulising and low frustration tolerance), and to teach the patient a set of appropriate rational beliefs.

For an exercise, work out what would be appropriate rational beliefs for a person with social phobia to acquire. The answers are at the end of this chapter.

Agoraphobia

Panic attacks, after a while, may occur in specific places or situations, such as crowds, queues and enclosed spaces, which limit a person's ability to move freely or to escape. In agoraphobia, these places become feared and avoided, and the person feels safest with a companion or in a familiar place, especially his or her home or car. Sometimes there is agoraphobia without panic disorder.

Generalized anxiety disorder (GAD)

'My life has been full of disasters and tragedies. Fortunately, almost none of them has happened.' GAD usually starts when a person is young, and is caused and characterised by worrying, that is, fortune-telling and catastrophising, predicting that things will go wrong, and worrying about possible ill health. Because of this, GAD sufferers are always anxious and hypervigilant.

Obsessive-compulsive disorder (OCD)

This condition is characterised by frequent obsessions and compulsions. Obsessions are recurrent, intrusive and persistent thoughts, images or impulses that the person considers to be stupid or repugnant.

Compulsions are mental or behavioural rituals that are stereotyped thoughts or actions which have the effect of temporarily reducing the anxiety caused by the obsessions.

Attempts to suppress or ignore the obsessions are usually ineffective. Somebody who is obsessed about contamination might wash his hands a hundred or more times a day. Someone else, worrying that the house might burn down, has to check up to 10 or 20 times that the stove is turned off before she can go to bed. An OCD sufferer may fear inadvertently causing harm to someone, or provoking some kind of bizarre or unspecified practically global misfortune if something isn't done just right. But like most other conditions, OCD can range in severity from being a minor irritation to having a major adverse effect on someone's life, even though the OCD sufferer knows that his fears are unrealistic.

Post-traumatic stress disorder (PTSD)

This condition is common enough to warrant mention. PTSD occurs after a person has been involved in or witnessed a fatal or life-threatening incident. It is more common in soldiers and people who live in violent places, but in our society PTSD can result from motor accidents, assaults, sexual assaults, and childhood abuse and sexual abuse. After a traumatic event, most people are disturbed, and find it hard to sleep for a few nights. More severe disturbance takes several weeks, or up to a couple of years, to settle spontaneously. If it lasts for longer than that, it will probably continue for decades or a lifetime, unless it is treated.

The main symptoms of PTSD are:

- re-experiencing the trauma spontaneously in nightmares and flashbacks, or when reminded of it;
- avoiding thinking, talking or reading about anything that reminds one of the trauma, or being in some places, for example passing the scene of one's motor accident;
- emotional flattening, detachment, loss of interest, and lack of a sense of a personal future;
- irritability and hypervigilance, and impaired sleep, concentration and memory.

Treatment of anxiety disorders

Any anxiety disorder should be treated unless it really is trivial. Without treatment it may last a lifetime. As long as an anxiety disorder exists, it increases the probability of developing some other condition, such as depression, and it certainly worsens the effects and the prognosis of performance anxiety.

In general, the main arm of treatment is cognitive behaviour therapy. Other psychological therapies, such as traditional 'dynamic' psychotherapy, can be helpful, but they are less efficient and slower than CBT. Counselling can help a person get through some general life problems, but is too vague and non-specific to be of any use in the treatment of anxiety disorders.

Medication

The modern antidepressants are not only effective in the treatment of depression, they also have a very important role to play in the treatment of all the anxiety disorders. For further information see Chapter 17.

Attention deficit disorder (ADD)

ADD can cause or intensify performance anxiety, so it is relevant to discuss it in this book.

ADD really does exist, and is a common condition, particularly in Australia and America. It is not caused by ingesting food colourings, but is a neurological disorder. Symptoms appear in early childhood, and it runs in some families. If hyperactivity is present, the condition is referred to as attention deficit/hyperactivity disorder (ADHD). The exact name is not important; what does matter is that the central problem is a reduced ability to sustain attention and concentration.

It can cause children (boys more often than girls) to be restless, impulsive, rowdy, easily distracted and distracting, or vague, daydreaming and forgetful. The vague and daydreaming group are not hyperactive. Despite the fact that many children with ADD are highly intelligent and creative, they usually underachieve, with a typical school term report saying, 'Freddy has plenty of ability, and would make good progress if he paid more attention in class, and handed his homework in on time.' Freddy's problems are boredom, scattered attention and procrastination.

These behavioural symptoms can have causes other than ADHD.

A few years of underachievement, failures, frequent criticism and critical labelling by others and himself create a negative self-image. Freddy learns to call himself 'stupid', 'idiot' and so on, and sees himself as unable to cope with much, because almost everything exceeds his meagre (he thinks) abilities.

ADD can persist into adulthood, when it can cause procrastinating, difficulty in organising and completing tasks, poor concentration, a tendency to make unplanned decisions, poor self-acceptance and depression-proneness.

I have had to treat several of my performance anxiety patients for ADD. These include postgraduate medical examination candidates and a 50-year-old opera singer who alerted me to his diagnosis by telling me that his poor concentration made it very hard for him to re-learn a role for a new production, when he had sung that part five or six times before in his career.

A common feature of ADHD is the ability to focus like a laser, almost obsessively, on something interesting, such as a game, hobby, or some creative pursuit. The absent-minded genius may not be a false stereotype, after all. This does not in any way weaken the diagnosis.

Treatment
ADHD is an organic condition caused by a deficiency of neuro-transmitter substances, mainly dopamine and noradrenaline, in an area in the brain. Some drugs, known as psycho-stimulants, increase the concentrations of these substances, and bring about feelings of calm, and improved mood, attention span and impulse control. It is rare for an ADD patient being treated with these drugs to abuse them. Perhaps this is because they do not experience a 'high', but feelings of calm, so there is no urge to increase the dose.

Answers to question on p. 168
- 'I like to be accepted and approved of, but there is no law that says it must happen.'
- 'My worth as a person is intrinsic to me and cannot be affected by whatever happens to me, including whether anyone accepts me or not.'
- 'When I meet people I may become anxious, but no matter how severe this is, it can never be too bad.'
- 'I can stand discomfort, including anxiety.'

---

17 Medication and other physical treatments

Although this book is about the cognitive therapy treatment of performance anxiety, you may need some basic information about medication and other non-psychological treatments.

First, a few general points:

- The one thing that works, that may fix the problem for good, is for a person to acquire a rational philosophy, and rational beliefs and self-talk about performance challenges.

- Other treatments may be useful temporarily, when one's coping abilities are not yet up to the task and need helping, or because the challenge is extremely strong.

- Conditions such as depression and attention deficit disorder usually need medication (and other treatments).

- Whether a medication is synthetic or 'natural' doesn't mean a thing. It is effective and safe, or it is not. With every medication (or treatment method), properly conducted clinical trials are needed to establish efficacy and safety.

- Thirty per cent of normal, sensible, people will respond to a dummy treatment as if it is an effective one. This is called the 'placebo response'. So an anecdotal report that one or two people responded to a certain treatment proves nothing, even though the treatment may actually be effective.

- Keep an open, sceptical, mind about any medication you are offered. Don't use a friend's medicine, as it may dangerously interact with something you are already taking, or exacerbate a medical condition.

Here is some brief, basic, information about orthodox medications. (For information on natural therapies, consult your library or nearest naturopath.)

SSRI (Selective Serotonin Reuptake Inhibitor) drugs are fluoxetine, fluvoxamine, sertraline, paroxetine and citalopram. They are effective (that is, they help most, but not all, cases) in treating depression, social phobia, panic attacks and OCD. They are safe, including in overdose, and never cause dependency, but their capacity for interacting with other medicines has to be kept in mind. They can have annoying but usually transient side-effects, such as headache, insomnia, nausea and diarrhoea. Sexual dysfunction is pretty frequent, and persistent. Weight gain is very infrequent, and sedation is uncommon.

SNRI (Serotonin and Noradrenaline Reuptake Inhibitor) drugs are very similar to the SSRIs.

Moclobemide is another modern drug used for treating depression and anxiety disorders.

The older antidepressants, namely the **tricyclics** (TCAs) and **monoamine oxidase inhibitors** (MAOIs) are just as effective, but have mostly been superseded because of more serious side-effects and lack of safety.

Benzodiazepines (Valium is the most familiar) effectively reduce anxiety, but they can cause mental slowing and reduced alertness, they provide only temporary symptomatic relief, and prolonged use can cause dependency. They can be useful, say in an emergency, in ameliorating extreme anxiety which would be far more performance-impairing than any side-effects of the medicine.

Beta blockers are anti-hypertensive drugs; think of them as anti-adrenalin drugs, as they reduce or abolish the palpitations and tremors of anxiety. They usually have no effect on mental functioning, but in some people they cause fuzziness. They are taken not regularly, but only in situations. Asthmatics should avoid them, as they can provoke asthma attacks.

Other treatments, such as yoga, meditation and massage, can induce a definite feeling of calm and wellbeing, but this will be of little or no help in a performance challenge, because they do nothing to change beliefs and self-talk.

18 General health and habits of life

You will find no surprises in this chapter. It consists of some commonsense advice, much of which you will know already, but a little reinforcement never hurts.

Nutrition

There is no need for a special diet; all you need do is to observe the principles of good nutrition. This means eating fresh fruit and vegetables every day, very limited amounts of meat, fresh fish if it's available, and not much fat or sugar. Limit alcohol to one or two drinks on three days of the week. Avoid extremes and zealotry.

Eat three or more regular meals a day, and avoid allowing yourself to become too hungry, as this can lead to bingeing.

Sleep

Get enough sleep. Recent research shows that even moderate sleep deprivation impairs cognitive performance to a measurable extent.

Exercise

Some people need no encouragement, and go into an acute withdrawal state if they don't get their daily exercise. They love being active, being on the move, and they love playing sports.

For the rest of us, it is recommended that we get 30 minutes of exercise (walking is fine) four or five times a week.

There are several benefits. Exercise improves cardiovascular fitness, and makes it easier to control one's weight. In addition, it has a mood-lifting effect because of the increased concentration of substances, known as endorphins, in the brain. Many people find that they are mentally sharper when they exercise regularly. People who are fit feel healthier, they can lose the muscular aches and pains of middle age, and they generally have more energy.

Drugs and medicines — prescribed and over-the-counter orthodox medications

If you are taking medicine, then it is reasonable, although not always correct, to presume that you need it, in which case you should feel and function better than if you are not taking it. But all medications have side-effects, and it is possible that what you take is causing lethargy, sedation or mental slowing. If this is how you feel, check with your doctor about your medication. You may do just as well on something that does not have those side-effects.

Recreational drugs

These include caffeine, alcohol, tobacco, marijuana, and hard drugs. We will have a brief look at each of these.

Caffeine can be a good pick-me-up — in moderation. More than three or four doses a day, and less if you are sensitive to it, can cause chronic anxiety and insomnia. If you are having trouble getting your anxiety levels down, then consider stopping caffeine altogether. But be warned — if you withdraw from caffeine, do so gradually, and avoid the withdrawal headache.

Alcohol can be good for the health, but only in strict moderation. Remember that a couple of drinks late at night can help you get to sleep, but will also diminish the quality of sleep or even cause rebound wakefulness in the middle of the night. This means starting the next day feeling and functioning below par.

Tobacco is smoked by some people for its relaxation effect. However, most smokers don't realise that this effect is very brief and is followed by increased levels of anxiety. It causes increased mental acuity and raised mood levels, but these benefits are outweighed by the risks to health. Most smokers would rather stop. Smoking cessation programs based on nicotine patches and behavioural counselling have a long-term success rate of 60 per cent. They are definitely worth trying.

Marijuana has a number of other names, including 'dope', which is quite appropriate. It certainly is relaxing, but it also causes loss of motivation and inertia. Some very heavy dope smokers function well in study and in intellectually demanding jobs, but it is hard to believe that they would not do better without it.

Hard drugs should be avoided at all costs. Their destructive effects on the minds, bodies and lives of people who are dependent on them are very well known. To be *dependent* on any substance, whether it be a hard or soft drug, legal or illegal, over-the-counter or prescribed, sedative, painkiller, mood-altering or hallucinogenic, can only make it harder, or impossible, to overcome performance anxiety, any benefits being only illusory or temporary.

Relationships and social life

It is possible to become obsessed with training, practising, studying, preparing for competition, or doing whatever is necessary in order to achieve one's reasonable goals. By 'obsession' I mean having the beliefs that lead one to think that everything else is of secondary importance. I have met many young people who say 'I don't have any time for a social life' or 'I have decided not to bother having a girlfriend/boyfriend for a couple of years, until I have finished my course.' They are being unnecessarily hard on themselves. Do they really believe that staying home seven nights a week, studying or practising the violin, is preferable to finding the time for some social life? They are, in fact, denying the facts of their human biology, which is that we humans are social beings who perform best, and enjoy life more, if we have friendships and close relationships. Loneliness is a very potent emotional poison. So what is actually going on here? The obsessive studier could be avoiding social relationships. If you are falling into the trap of obsession and irrational self-denial and isolation, recognise now that it is harmful, that it is imposing a high cost upon you, and that there are no benefits, including the fact that your performance will definitely not be improved.

If your goals are very important to you, then you will almost certainly have to make an effort and practise some self-denial, at least for a while and to some degree (high frustration tolerance).

However, social isolation and lack of stimulation and variety in one's life lead to boredom, which is depressing, reduces motivation, and increases the likelihood of giving up. A very clear example of this is in the case of young competitive swimmers, whose lives consist of nothing at all except school, swimming, training, homework and sleep. Many of them become extremely fed up with this demanding and restrictive way of life.

If this is your problem, start looking for the self-talk that is leading to the obsessive behaviour. Dispute it, evolve some rational self-talk to replace the irrational, and set about changing your behaviour patterns.

The most likely causes of this obsessive behaviour are perfectionistic fears of failure, the need to be approved of, social phobia, or a personality trait.

If your relationships with others are not as smooth as you would like them to be, and you think that you are getting more distress and conflict and less satisfaction than you would think is reasonable, don't automatically assume that it is everybody else's fault. Are your conflict-resolution skills satisfactory, or do you find when you try to negotiate with people that it breaks down too easily? Are you able to assert yourself as comfortably and as often as you would like to? Do you bottle everything up?

Problems with assertiveness and anger lead to chronic stress if they are not resolved. Young people sharing houses fairly often find that instead of cooperation and harmony there is a degree of tension and resentment. You don't have to love your companions; mutual respect will be enough.

19 The Quick Fix

Although this book is intended for people with a problem with performance anxiety, we have to be realistic, and acknowledge that some people reading this book may soon be facing an examination, an audition or a contest. This allows no time for fundamental change. Nevertheless, given determination and the ability to work hard at the Quick Fix methods described in this chapter, the performance-anxious person can still expect to be helped.

Identifying areas of vulnerability

It is important to recognise your problem areas, so they can be efficiently targeted for change. There are some problems that need to be identified early, because if they exist and are not recognised or dealt with, they will hinder your efforts to overcome your performance anxiety.

If you discover in the course of reading the next few pages, that you have particular problems with one or two of the irrational beliefs or behaviour patterns, do not just concentrate on them. Attend to all aspects of your irrational beliefs and actions, with a stronger focus where it is appropriate.

The following questionnaire will help you identify your irrational beliefs. This is not a diagnostic test, but a guide.

For each statement answer 'yes' if you recall having thought that way in the last six months, or 'no' if this is not the case.

	Yes	No
1. I have to succeed at, or win, any worthwhile thing I attempt.	☐	☐
2. People have to be impressed by my efforts.	☐	☐
3. There are standards for how people should behave, and they must stick to them.	☐	☐
4. I should be able to compete or perform without having to be nervous as well.	☐	☐
5. When I try, and don't succeed, it's not just bad, it's horrible.	☐	☐
6. It's more than disappointing when I don't succeed — it's unbearable.	☐	☐
7. I feel like a failure when I don't perform well.	☐	☐
8. I must never fail at anything.	☐	☐
9. What people think of my performance is extremely important to me.	☐	☐
10. Everyone must always strive to do their best.	☐	☐
11. I can't accept the idea that talent isn't enough, and that I have to work hard and be patient.	☐	☐
12. It's a horrible experience when people aren't impressed with my efforts, or when they don't understand or appreciate what I do.	☐	☐
13. I can't stand it when my efforts are not appreciated or properly judged, or when people do not like what I do.	☐	☐
14. If I don't perform well enough, it means I am below standard.	☐	☐
15. I always strive to do my best, because I have to.	☐	☐
16. People's judgement of my efforts is crucial to me.	☐	☐
17. People must do the right thing at all times. If you don't, it is not good enough.	☐	☐

	Yes	No

18. Having anxiety symptoms when I am competing or performing is not how it should be. I should be calm. ☐ ☐

19. It is awful to have anxiety symptoms when I am performing or competing. ☐ ☐

20. I can't bear feeling as nervous as I do when I am performing. ☐ ☐

21. Show me a runner-up and I'll show you a loser. ☐ ☐

22. Giving an average performance is not good enough for me; I have to do really well. ☐ ☐

23. If someone is unimpressed with my performance, that is unacceptable to me. ☐ ☐

24. There is no excuse for someone not doing the very best they can. ☐ ☐

25. It should be better than this — considering all the effort, obstacles, waiting and discomfort. ☐ ☐

26. It's dreadful having to go through practising, waiting, hassles and discomforts, in order to achieve my goal. ☐ ☐

27. All that I have to go through in order to reach my goals — I can't stand it. ☐ ☐

28. If I can't control how I feel when I am performing or competing, it proves I am incompetent. ☐ ☐

In each category mentioned below:
- One 'yes' response = you probably do not have a problem in this area.
- Two or three 'yes' responses = you need to read the relevant chapters.
- Four 'yes' responses = focus on this belief as a definite problem area.

Statements 1, 8, 15 and 22 refer to demands on oneself to succeed (see Chapter 7).

Statements 2, 9, 16, and 23 refer to demands on oneself to gain approval (see Chapter 8).

Statements 3, 10, 17, and 24 refer to demands on others to behave competently and correctly (see Chapter 9).

Statements 4, 11, 18, and 25 refer to demands that life be easy, comfortable and certain (see Chapter 10).

Statements 5, 12, 19 and 26 refer to awfulising (see Chapter 11).

Statements 6, 13, 20, and 27 refer to I-can't-stand-it-itis, or low frustration tolerance (see Chapter 11).

Questions 7, 14, 21, and 28 refer to global rating of self and others (see Chapter 12).

The following questions are about whether you procrastinate too much.

	Yes	No
1. I put some things off, but it's never a real problem.	☐	☐
2. Sometimes I wish I didn't procrastinate as much as I do.	☐	☐
3. My procrastinating sometimes causes me real distress and inconvenience.	☐	☐
4. My procrastinating is a major problem in my life.	☐	☐

If you answered YES to questions 3 or 4, you will need to tackle procrastinating as a problem in its own right.

Chapter 13 is an introduction to the causes and remedies of procrastinating. But if you are a hardcore procrastinator read the recommended book (*Do It Now* — see Bibliography), or seek professional help.

How to help yourself in a short time

If you have performance anxiety, and are reading the quick fix section of this book to help you perform very soon, some of the techniques described in the book have been abbreviated here, designed for this purpose, and can certainly be helpful to you now.

1. Identify your area(s) of vulnerability (see questionnaire, p 178–79) and go to the chapters that relate to them.
2. Read the chapters' disputations and memorise the rational beliefs (at the end of each chapter) that could be helpful to

you. To help remember them, put red stickers on places such as the refrigerator, your watch, the car steering wheel. When you see a sticker, recite the rational belief(s) to yourself.

3. Daily, practise whatever form of relaxation/s suits you best.
4. Practise rational-emotive imagery, in its positive and negative forms as described in Chapter 15. The technique, and others, can be highly effective and valuable at coaching you in how to think and feel when you confront your imminent challenge. Practise many times a day.
5. Learn self-instructional braining (Chapter 15) and construct your own set of instructions. This technique will help you to focus on what you have to do right now, as well as in the time leading up to, during, and after your performance/challenge.

The Critic

When you don't have much time to prepare for a performance/challenge, be aware that your Critic is almost certain to attack you. So prepare yourself for this. Read about it in Chapter 15.

If we make the assumption that you have a performance to deal with in two weeks or so, focus on the 'Blast-back treatment'. Shout and scream (inside your head) the worst possible abuse you can think of at the critic. During this period, don't waste time. Start reciting your favourite rational statements or your coping self-instructional statements. Perhaps a positive rational-emotive imagery could be more helpful. Experiment. One coping method may be more useful to you than another right now. Find it and use it.

Worry management

Frequently write up a worry management risk estimation (Chapter 15). This technique helps to pin worries down, and suggests practical tactics to take the steam out of them.

Finally

Like so many people, you have endured the torment of performance anxiety. Perhaps your performance anxiety has been career-related and very important to you. Perhaps it occurs in social or seemingly trivial situations. Performance anxiety casts a wide net. The details do not matter. What does matter is that you have suffered enough.

Now, it's different; you know what to do — how to identify your faulty beliefs, how to demolish them and how to train yourself to think rationally, to enjoy trying, to prefer and love succeeding, to stand failure, to dread nothing, and always to know that whatever happens, you are a worthwhile human being.

Bibliography

Orlick, Terry, *In Pursuit of Excellence: How to Win in Sport and Life Through Mental Training*, 3rd edn, Human Kinetics Publishers, Inc., Champaign, Illinois, 2000.

Burns, David D. MD, *Feeling Good: The New Mood Therapy*, Morrow, William & Co., New York, 1999.

Knaus, Dr William J. *Do It Now! Break the Procrastination Habit*, rev. edition, John Wiley & Sons, Inc., New York, 1998.

McKay, Matthew, and Fanning, Patrick, *Self-Esteem: A Proven Program of Cognitive Techniques for Assessing, Improving and Maintaining Your Self-Esteem*, 3rd edn, New Harbinger Publications, Oakland, California, 2000.

Ellis, A. and Harper, R., *A New Guide to Rational Living*, Prentice Hall, Eaglewood Cliffs, New Jersey, 1975.

McKay, Matthew, Davis, Martha, and Fanning, Patrick, *Thoughts and Feelings: Taking Control of Your Moods and Your Life*, New Harbinger Publications, Oakland, California, 1997.

Index